DATA MINING AND BUSINESS INTELLIGENCE

DM&BI

DR. GAURAV KUMAR AMETA

Made with ♥ on the Notion Press Platform
www.notionpress.com

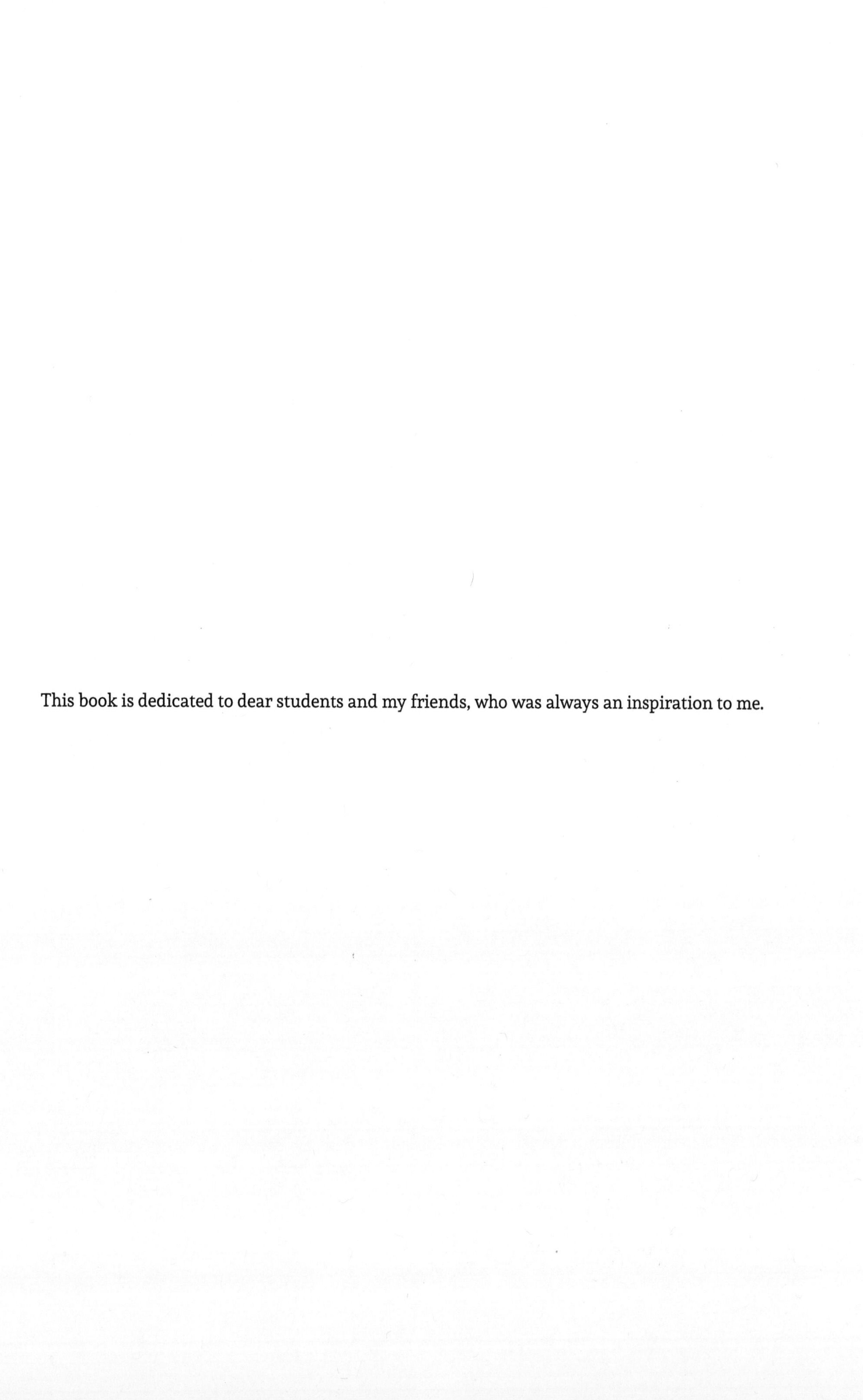

This book is dedicated to dear students and my friends, who was always an inspiration to me.

Contents

PREFACE

In this book has developed from my own class notes. It reflects many years of CSE&IT industry experience, as well as many years of academic teaching experience. The chapters are organized for a typical semester graduate course. The book contains caselets from real-world information at the beginning of every chapter.

Acknowledgements

Business is the act of doing something productive to serve someone need, and thus earn a living, and make the world a better place. Business activities are recorded on paper or using electronic media, and then these records become data. There is more data from customers' responses and on the industry as a whole. All this data can be analyzed and mined using special tools and techniques to generate patterns and intelligence, which reflect how the business is functioning. These ideas can then be fed back into the business so that it can evolve to become more effective and efficient in serving customer needs.

I

Introduction to Data Warehousing and Business Intelligence

What is Data Warehouse? Explain it with Key Feature.

Data warehousing provides architectures and tools for business executives to systematically organize, understand, and use their data to make strategic decisions.

A data warehouse refers to a database that is maintained separately from an organization's operational databases.

Data warehouse systems allow for the integration of a variety of application systems.

They support information processing by providing a solid platform of consolidated historical data for analysis.

According to William H. Inmon, a leading architect in the construction of data warehouse systems, "A data warehouse is a subject-oriented, integrated, time-variant, and nonvolatile collection of data in support of management's decision making process"

The four keywords, subject-oriented, integrated, time-variant, and nonvolatile, distinguish data warehouses from other data repository systems, such as relational database systems, transaction processing systems, and file systems.

Subject-oriented:

A data warehouse is organized around major subjects, such as customer, supplier, product, and sales.

Rather than concentrating on the day-to-day operations and transaction processing of an organization, a data warehouse focuses on the modeling and analysis of data for decision makers.

Data warehouses typically provide a simple and concise view around particular subject issues by excluding data that are not useful in the decision support process.

Integrated:

A data warehouse is usually constructed by integrating multiple heterogeneous sources, such as relational databases, flat files, and on-line transaction records.

Data cleaning and data integration techniques are applied to ensure consistency in naming conventions, encoding structures, attribute measures, and so on.

Time-variant:

Data are stored to provide information from a historical perspective (e.g., the past 5–10 years).

Every key structure in the data warehouse contains, either implicitly or explicitly, an element of time.

Nonvolatile:

A data warehouse is always a physically separate store of data transformed from the application data found in the operational environment.

Due to this separation, a data warehouse does not require transaction processing, recovery, and concurrency control mechanisms.

It usually requires only two operations in data accessing: initial loading of data and access of data.

Explain Data Warehouse Design Process in Detail.

A data warehouse can be built using a top-down approach, a bottom-up approach, or a combination of both.

Top Down Approach

The top-down approach starts with the overall design and planning.

It is useful in cases where the technology is mature and well known, and where the business problems that must be solved are clear and well understood.

Bottom up Approach

The bottom-up approach starts with experiments and prototypes.

This is useful in the early stage of business modeling and technology development.

It allows an organization to move forward at considerably less expense and to evaluate the benefits of the technology before making significant commitments.

Combined Approach

In the combined approach, an organization can exploit the planned and strategic nature of the top-down approach while retaining the rapid implementation and opportunistic application of the bottom-up approach.

The warehouse design process consists of the following steps:

Choose a business process to model, for example, orders, invoices, shipments, inventory, account administration, sales, or the general ledger.

If the business process is organizational and involves multiple complex object collections, a data warehouse model should be followed. However, if the process is departmental and focuses on the analysis of one kind of business process, a data mart model should be chosen.

Choose the grain of the business process. The grain is the fundamental, atomic level of data to be represented in the fact table for this process, for example, individual transactions, individual daily snapshots, and so on.

Choose the dimensions that will apply to each fact table record. Typical dimensions are time, item, customer, supplier, warehouse, transaction type, and status.

Choose the measures that will populate each fact table record. Typical measures are numeric additive quantities like dollars sold and units sold.

3) What is Business Intelligence? Explain Business Intelligence in today's perspective.

While there are varying definitions for BI, Forrester defines it broadly as a "set of methodologies, processes, architectures, and technologies that transform raw data into meaningful and useful information that allows business users to make informed business decisions with real-time data that can put a company ahead of its competitors".

In other words, the high-level goal of BI is to help a business user turn business-related data into actionable knowledge.

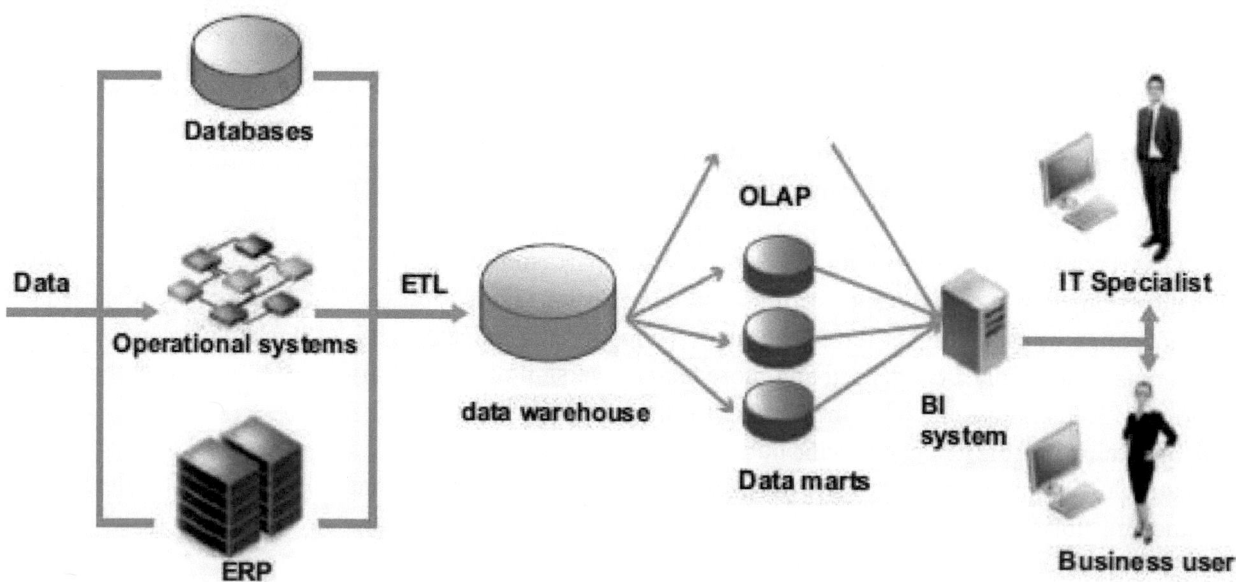

BI traditionally focused on reports, dashboards, and answering predefined questions

Today BI also includes a focus on deeper, exploratory, and interactive analyses of the data using Business Analytics such as data mining, predictive analytics, statistical analysis, and natural language processing solutions.

BI systems evolved by adding layers of data staging to increase the accessibility of the business data to business users.

Data from the operational systems and ERP were extracted, transformed into a more consumable form (e.g., column names labeled for human rather than computer consumption, errors corrected, duplication eliminated).

Data from a warehouse were then loaded into OLAP cubes, as well as data marts stored in data warehouses.

OLAP cubes facilitated the analysis of data over several dimensions.

Data marts present a subset of the data in the warehouse, tailored to a specific line of business.

Using Business Intelligence, the business user, with the help of an IT specialist who had set up the system for her, could now more easily access and analyze the data through a BI system.

Meta data repository

Metadata are data about data. When used in a data warehouse, metadata are the data that define warehouse objects.

Metadata are created for the data names and definitions of the given warehouse.

Additional metadata are created and captured for time stamping any extracted data, the source of the extracted data, and missing fields that have been added by data cleaning or integration processes.

A metadata repository should contain the following:

A description of the structure of the data warehouse, which includes the warehouse schema, view, dimensions, hierarchies, and derived data definitions, as well as data mart locations and contents.

Operational metadata, which include data lineage (history of migrated data and the sequence of transformations applied to it), currency of data (active, archived, or purged), and monitoring information (warehouse usage statistics, error reports, and audit trails).

The algorithms used for summarization, which include measure and dimension definition algorithms, data on granularity, partitions, subject areas, aggregation, summarization and predefined queries and reports.

The mapping from the operational environment to the data warehouse, which includes source databases and their contents, gateway descriptions, data partitions, data extraction, cleaning, transformation rules and defaults, data refresh and purging rules, and security (user authorization and access control).

Data related to system performance, which include indices and profiles that improve data access and retrieval performance, in addition to rules for the timing and scheduling of refresh, update, and replication cycles.

Business metadata, which include business terms and definitions, data ownership information, and charging policies.

What do you mean by data mart? What are the different types of data mart?

Data marts contain a subset of organization-wide data that is valuable to specific groups of people in an organization.

A data mart contains only those data that is specific to a particular group.

Data marts improve end-user response time by allowing users to have access to the specific type of data they need to view most often by providing the data in a way that supports the collective view of a group of users.

A data mart is basically a condensed and more focused version of a data warehouse that reflects the regulations and process specifications of each business unit within an organization.

Each data mart is dedicated to a specific business function or region.

For example, the marketing data mart may contain only data related to items, customers, and sales. Data marts are confined to subjects.

Listed below are the reasons to create a data mart:

To speed up the queries by reducing the volume of data to be scanned.

To partition data in order to impose access control strategies.

To segment data into different hardware platforms.

Easy access to frequently needed data

Creates collective view by a group of users

Improves end-user response time

Lower cost than implementing a full data warehouse

Contains only business essential data and is less cluttered.

Three basic types of data marts are dependent, independent, and hybrid.

The categorization is based primarily on the data source that feeds the data mart.

Dependent data marts draw data from a central data warehouse that has already been created.

Independent data marts, in contrast, are standalone systems built by drawing data directly from operational or external sources of data or both.

Hybrid data marts can draw data from operational systems or data warehouses

Dependent Data Marts

A dependent data mart allows you to unite your organization's data in one data warehouse.

This gives you the usual advantages of centralization.

Figure illustrates a dependent data mart.

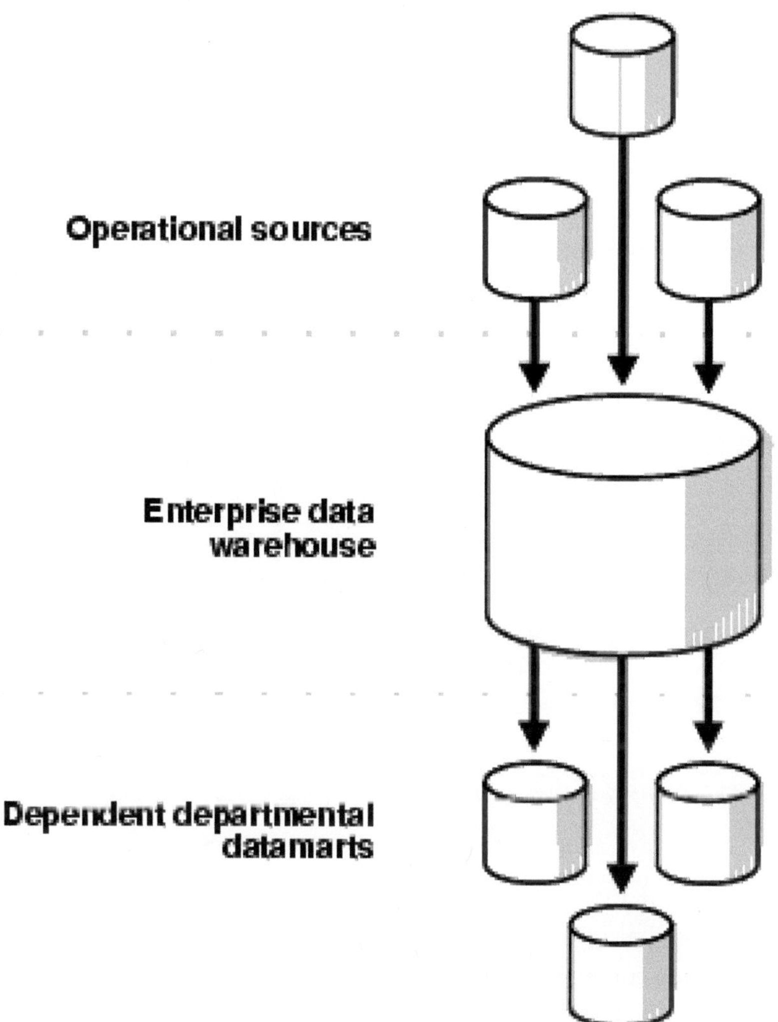

2. Independent Data Marts

An independent data mart is created without the use of a central data warehouse.
This could be desirable for smaller groups within an organization.
Figure illustrates an independent data mart.

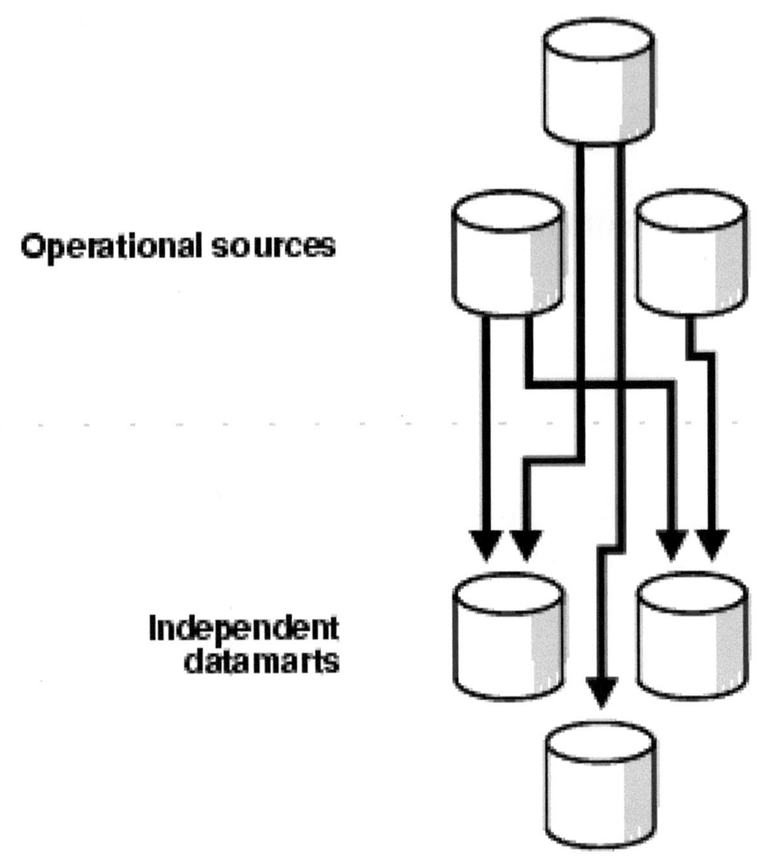

3. Hybrid Data Marts

A hybrid data mart allows you to combine input from sources other than a data warehouse.

This could be useful for many situations, especially when you need ad hoc integration, such as after a new group or product is added to the organization.

Figure illustrates a hybrid data mart.

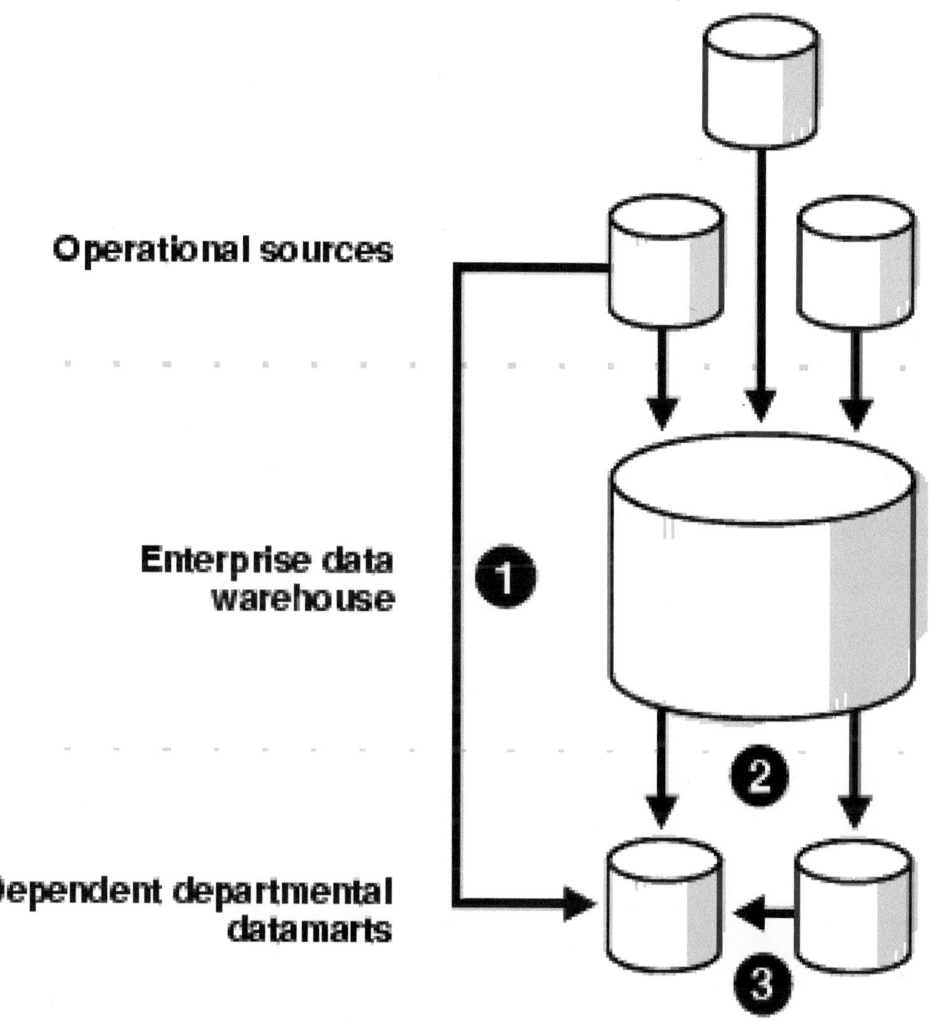

Data warehousing for information processing, analytical processing, and data Mining.

Data warehouses are used in a wide range of applications for Business executives to perform data analysis and make strategic decisions.

In many firms, data warehouses are used as an integral part of a plan-execute-assess "closed-loop" feedback system for enterprise management.

Data warehouses are used extensively in banking and financial services, consumer goods and retail distribution sectors, and controlled manufacturing, such as demand based production.

Business users need to have the means to know what exists in the data warehouse (through metadata), how to access the contents of the data warehouse, how to examine the contents using analysis tools, and how to present the results of such analysis.

There are three kinds of data warehouse applications:

Information processing

It supports querying, basic statistical analysis, and reporting using crosstabs, tables, charts, or graphs.

A current trend in data warehouse information processing is to construct low-cost Web-based accessing tools that are then integrated with Web browsers.

Information processing, based on queries, can find useful information. However, answers to such queries reflect the information directly stored in databases or computable by aggregate functions.

They do not reflect sophisticated patterns or regularities buried in the database. Therefore, information processing is not data mining.

Analytical processing

It supports basic OLAP operations, including slice-and-dice, drill-down, roll-up, and pivoting.

It generally operates on historical data in both summarized and detailed forms.

The major strength of on-line analytical processing over information processing is the multidimensional data analysis of data warehouse data.

It can derive information summarized at multiple granularities from user-specified subsets of a data warehouse.

Data mining

It supports knowledge discovery by finding hidden patterns and associations, constructing analytical models, performing classification and prediction, and presenting the mining results using visualization tools.

It may analyze data existing at more detailed granularities than the summarized data provided in a data warehouse.

It may also analyze transactional, spatial, textual, and multimedia data that are difficult to model with current multidimensional database technology.

II

The Architecture of BI and Data Warehouse

Explain three tier data warehouse architecture in brief.

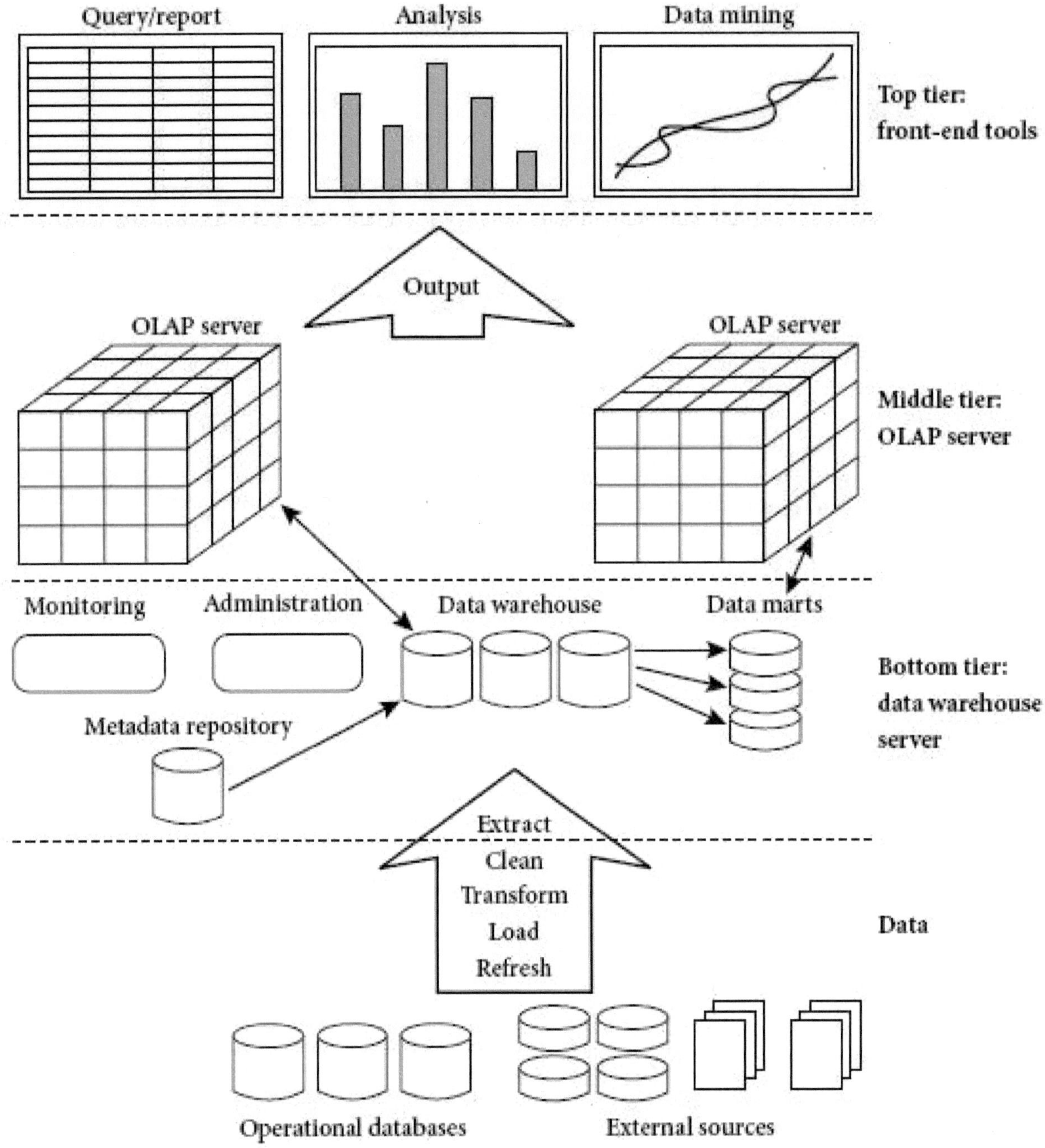

Bottom tier:

The bottom tier is a warehouse database server that is almost always a relational database system.

Back-end tools and utilities are used to feed data into the bottom tier from operational databases or other external sources.

These tools and utilities perform data extraction, cleaning, and transformation, as well as load and refresh functions to update the data warehouse.

The data are extracted using application program interfaces known as gateways.

A gateway is supported by the underlying DBMS and allows client programs to generate SQL code to be executed at a server.

Examples of gateways include ODBC (Open Database Connection) and OLEDB (Open Linking and Embedding for Databases) by Microsoft and JDBC (Java Database Connection).

This tier also contains a metadata repository, which stores information about the data warehouse and its contents.

Middle tier:

The middle tier is an OLAP server that is typically implemented using either.

A relational OLAP (ROLAP) model, that is, an extended relational DBMS that maps operations on multidimensional data to standard relational operations or,

A multidimensional OLAP (MOLAP) model, that is, a special-purpose server that directly implements multidimensional data and operations.

Top tier:

The top tier is a front-end client layer, which contains query and reporting tools, analysis tools, and/or data mining tools.

From the architecture point of view, there are three data warehouse models:

Enterprise warehouse:

An enterprise warehouse collects all of the information about subjects spanning the entire organization.

It provides corporate-wide data integration, usually from one or more operational systems or external information providers, and is cross-functional in scope.

It typically contains detailed data as well as summarized data,

It can range in size from a few gigabytes to hundreds of gigabytes, terabytes, or beyond.

Data mart:

A data mart contains a subset of corporate-wide data that is of value to a specific group of users.

Virtual warehouse:

A virtual warehouse is a set of views over operational databases.

For efficient query processing, only some of the possible summary views may be materialized.

Differentiate between OLTP and OLAP systems.

Feature	OLTP	OLAP
Characteristic	operational processing	informational processing
Orientation	transaction	analysis
User	clerk, DBA, database professional	knowledge worker (e.g., manager, executive, analyst)
Function	day-to-day operations	long-term informational requirements, decision support
DB design	ER based, application-oriented	star/snowflake, subject-oriented
Data	current; guaranteed up-to-date	historical; accuracy maintained over time
Summarization	primitive, highly detailed	summarized, consolidated
View	detailed, flat relational	summarized, multidimensional

Unit of work	short, simple transaction	complex query
Access	read/write	mostly read
Focus	data in	information out
Operations	index/hash on primary key	lots of scans
No. of records accessed	tens	millions
Number of users	thousands	hundreds
DB size	100 MB to GB	100 GB to TB
Priority	high performance, high availability	high flexibility, end-user autonomy
Metric	transaction throughput	query throughput, response time

Application of concept hierarchy?

A concept hierarchy defines a sequence of mappings from a set of low-level concepts to higher-level, more general concepts.

Consider a concept hierarchy for the dimension location. City values for location include Vancouver, Toronto, New York, and Chicago.

Each city, however, can be mapped to the province or state to which it belongs.

For example, Vancouver can be mapped to British Columbia, and Chicago to Illinois.

The provinces and states can in turn be mapped to the country to which they belong, such as Canada or the USA.

These mappings form a concept hierarchy for the dimension location, mapping a set of low-level concepts (i.e., cities) to higher-level, more general concepts (i.e., countries).

The concept hierarchy described above is illustrated in following Figure.

Concept hierarchies may be provided manually by system users, domain experts, or knowledge engineers, or may be automatically generated based on statistical analysis of the data distribution.

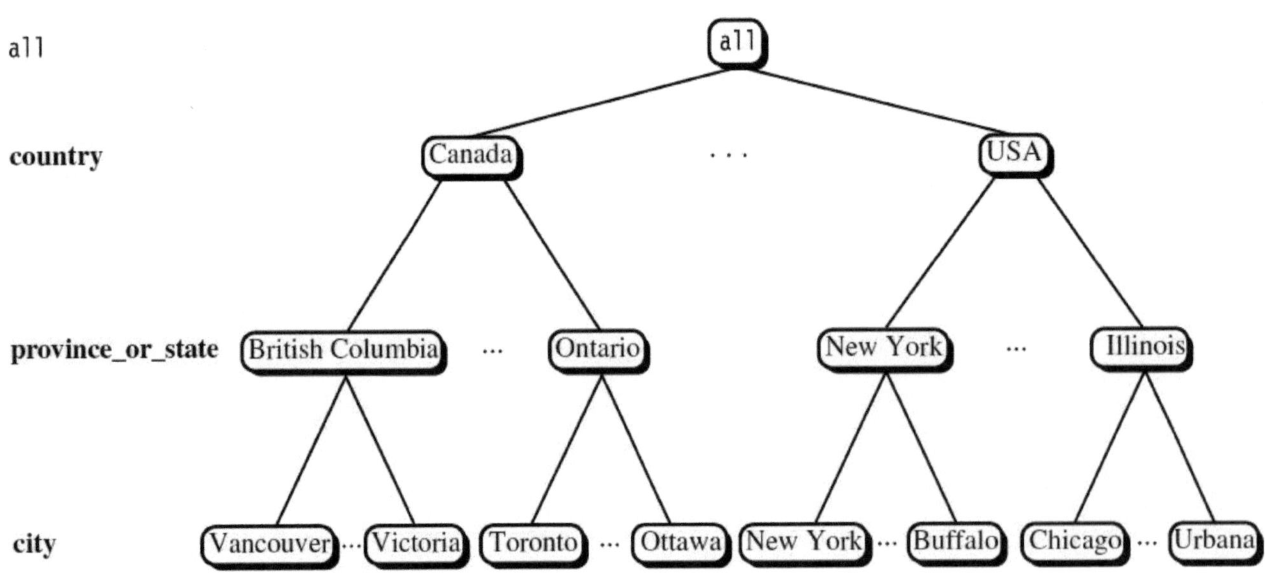

Many concept hierarchies are implicit within the database schema.

For example, suppose that the dimension location is described by the attributes number, street, city, province or state, zipcode, and country.

These attributes are related by a total order, forming a concept hierarchy such as "street < city < province or state < country". This hierarchy is shown in following Figure (a).

Alternatively, the attributes of a dimension may be organized in a partial order, forming a lattice.

An example of a partial order for the time dimension based on the attributes day, week, month, quarter, and year is "day <{ month <quarter; week} < year". This lattice structure is shown in Figure (b).

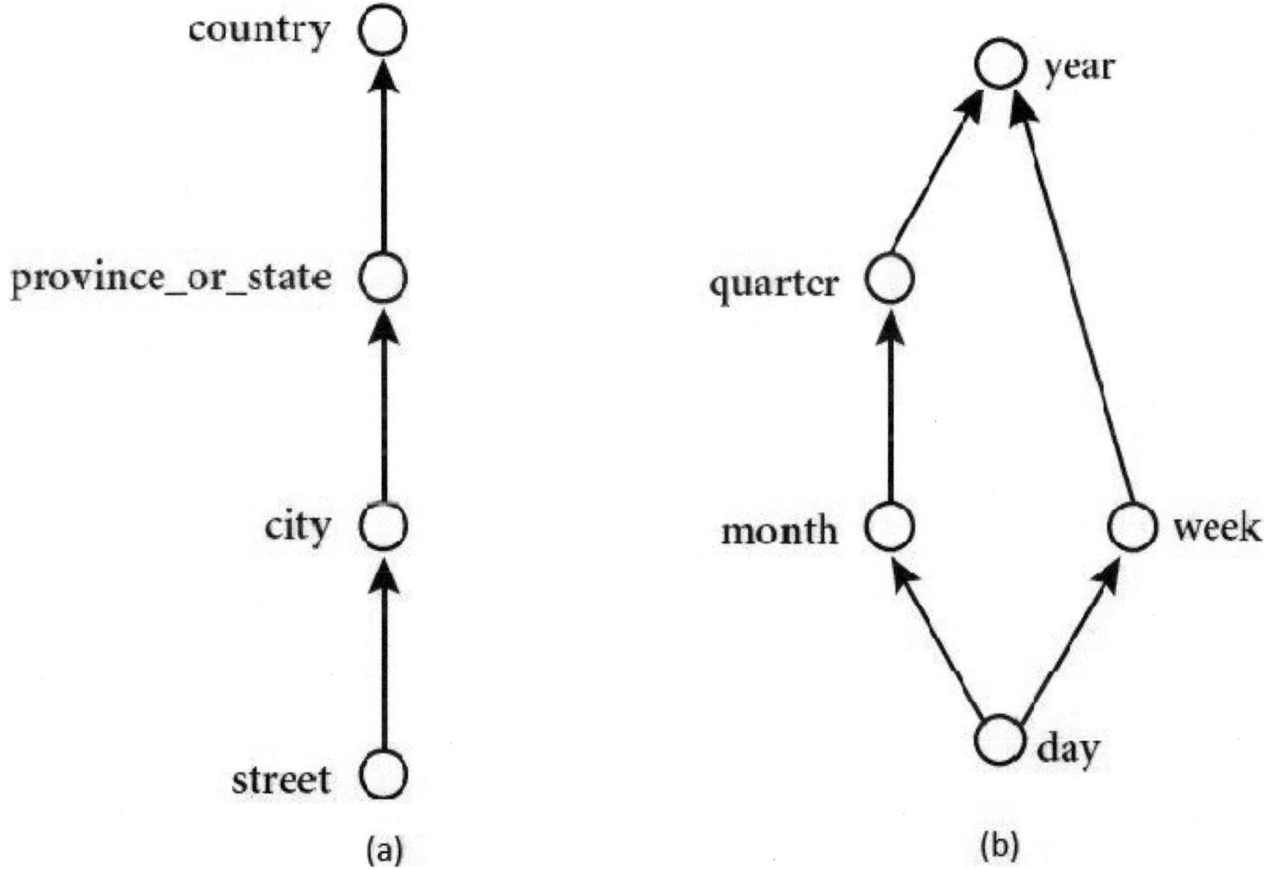

A concept hierarchy that is a total or partial order among attributes in a database schema is called a schema hierarchy.

Concept hierarchies may also be defined by discretizing or grouping values for a given dimension or attribute, resulting in a set-grouping hierarchy.

A total or partial order can be defined among groups of values.

There may be more than one concept hierarchy for a given attribute or dimension, based on different user viewpoints.

Design methods for multidimensional database: Star schema, Snowflake schema, Fact constellation schema. Also compare them with illustration.

The entity-relationship data model is commonly used in the design of relational databases, where a database schema consists of a set of entities and the relationships between them.

Such a data model is appropriate for on-line transaction processing.

A data warehouse, however, requires a concise, subject-oriented schema that facilitates on-line data analysis.

The most popular data model for a data warehouse is a multidimensional model.

Such a model can exist in the form of a star schema, a snowflake schema, or a fact constellation schema.

a large central table (fact table) containing the bulk of the data, with no redundancy, and

a set of smaller attendant tables (dimension tables), one for each dimension.

The schema graph resembles a starburst, with the dimension tables displayed in a radial pattern around the central fact table.

DMQL code for star schema can be written as follows:

Let's look at each of these schema types.

Star schema: The most common modeling paradigm is the star schema, in which the data warehouse contains,

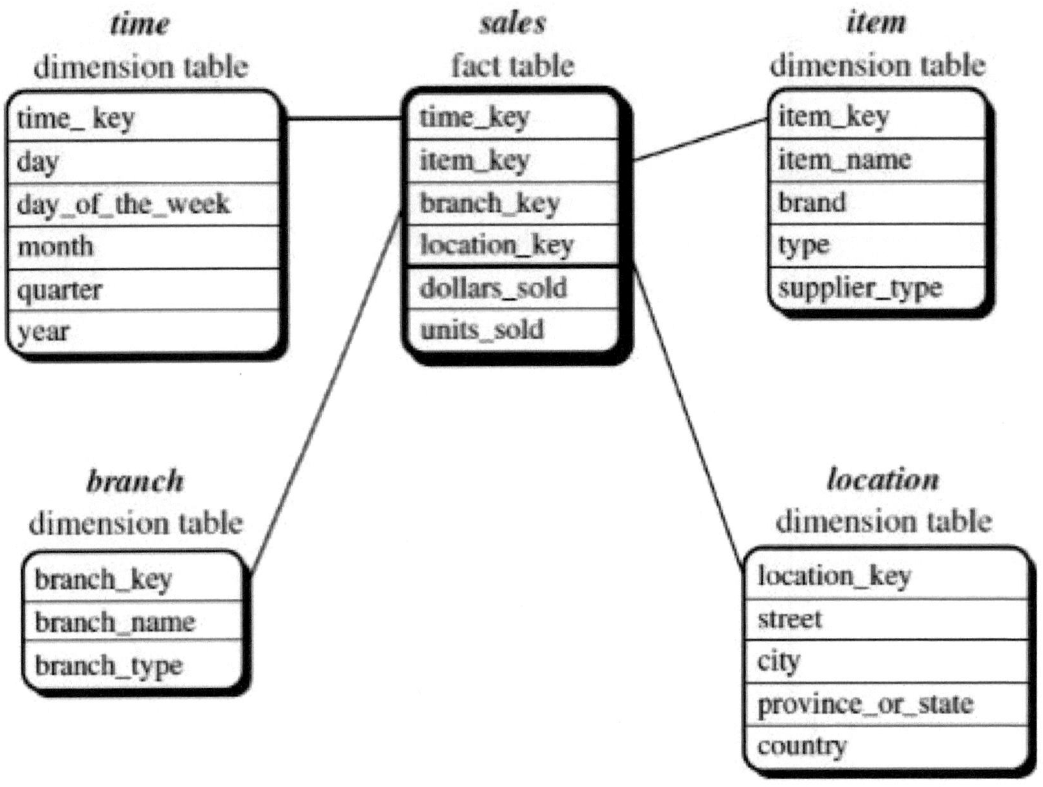

define cube sales star [time, item, branch, location]:

dollars sold = sum(sales in dollars), units sold = count(*)

define dimension time as (time key, day, day of week, month, quarter, year) define dimension item as (item key, item name, brand, type, supplier type) define dimension branch as (branch key, branch name, branch type)

define dimension location as (location key, street, city, province or state, country)

Snowflake shema: The major difference between the snowflake and star schema models is that the dimension tables of the snowflake model may be kept in normalized form to reduce redundancies. Such a table is easy to maintain and saves storage space.

However, this saving of space is negligible in comparison to the typical magnitude of the fact table. Furthermore, the snowflake structure can reduce the effectiveness of browsing, since more joins will be needed to execute a query.

Hence, although the snowflake schema reduces redundancy, it is not as popular as the star schema in data warehouse design.

DMQL code for star schema can be written as follows:

define cube sales snowflake [time, item, branch, location]: dollars sold = sum(sales in dollars), units sold = count(*)

define dimension time as (time key, day, day of week, month, quarter, year) define dimension item as (item key, item name, brand, type, supplier (supplier key, supplier type))

define dimension branch as (branch key, branch name, branch type) define dimension location as (location key, street, city

(city key, city, province or state, country))

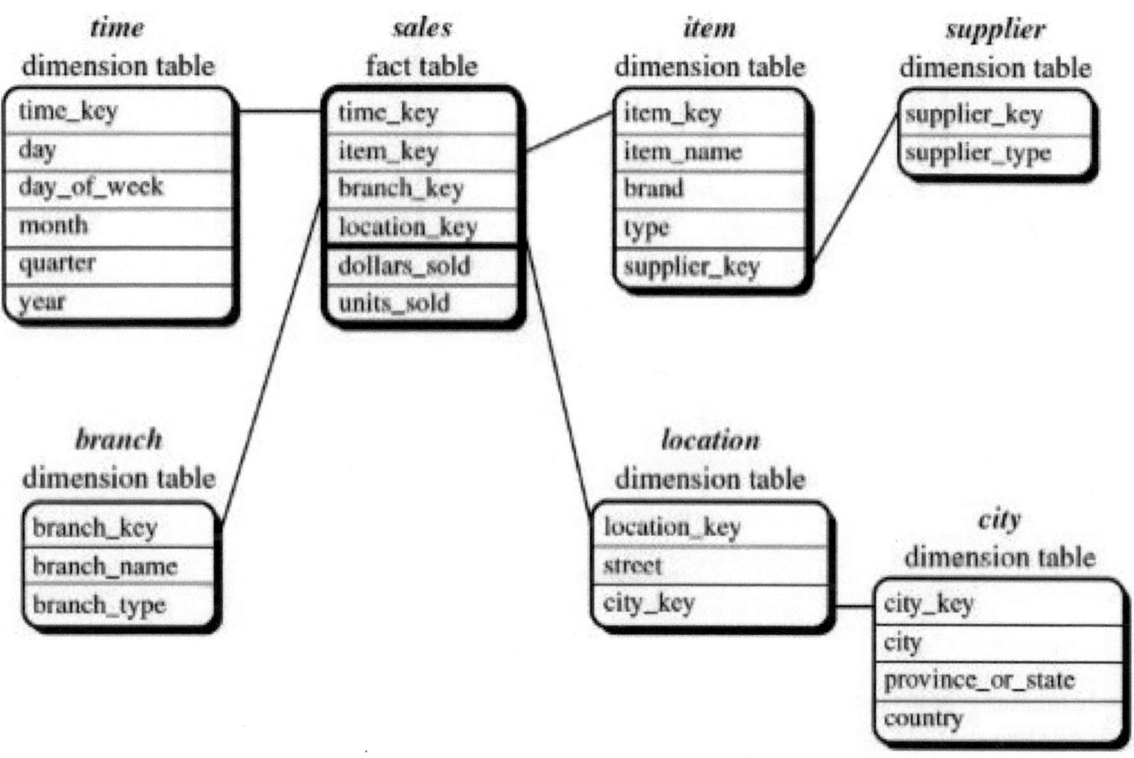

Fact constellation: Sophisticated applications may require multiple fact tables to share dimension tables.

This kind of schema can be viewed as a collection of stars, and hence is called a galaxy schema or a fact constellation.

A fact constellation schema allows dimension tables to be shared between fact tables.

For example, the dimensions tables for time, item, and location are shared between both the sales and shipping fact tables.

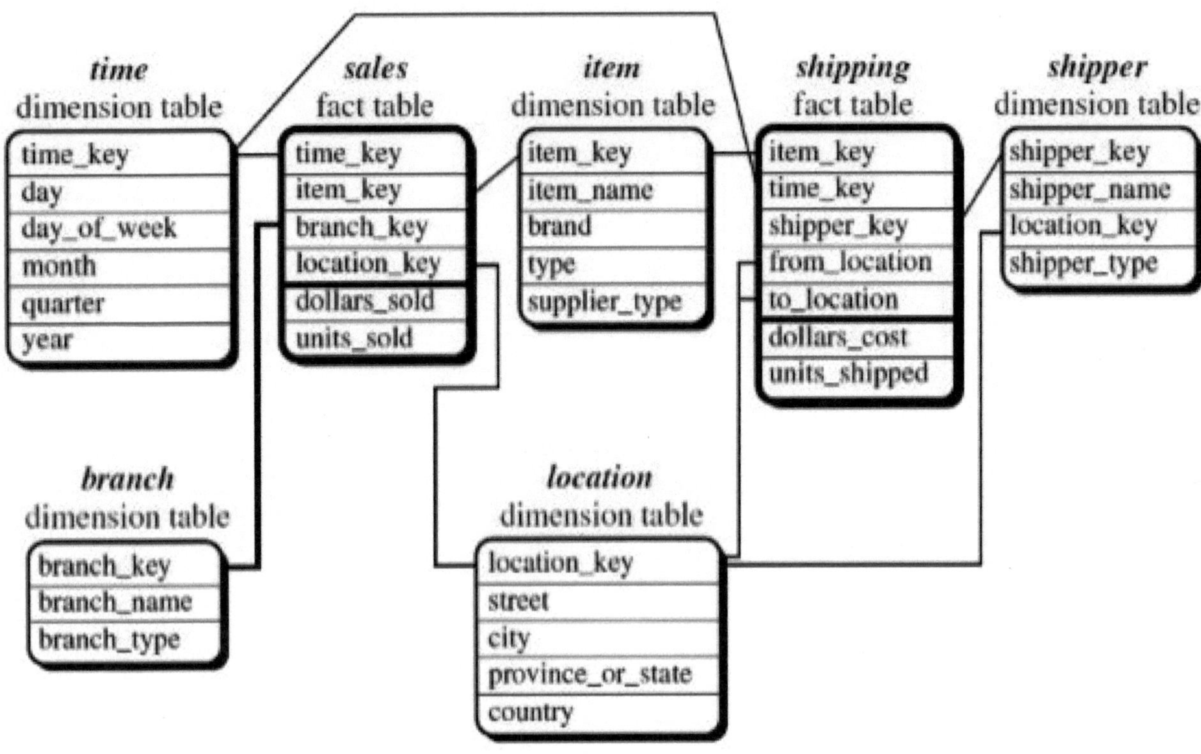

DMQL code for star schema can be written as follows:

Explain OLAP Operations in the Multidimensional Data Model?

Roll-upRoll-up performs aggregation on a data cube in any of the following ways:

By climbing up a concept hierarchy for a dimension

By dimension reduction

The following diagram illustrates how roll-up works.

define cube sales [time, item, branch, location]:

dollars sold = sum(sales in dollars), units sold = count(*)

define dimension time as (time key, day, day of week, month, quarter, year) define dimension item as (item key, item name, brand, type, supplier type) define dimension branch as (branch key, branch name, branch type)

define dimension location as (location key, street, city, province or state, country)

define cube shipping [time, item, shipper, from location, to location]: dollars cost = sum(cost in dollars), units shipped = count(*)

define dimension time as time in cube sales define dimension item as item in cube sales

define dimension shipper as (shipper key, shipper name, location as location in cube sales, shipper type)

define dimension from location as location in cube sales define dimension to location as location in cube sales

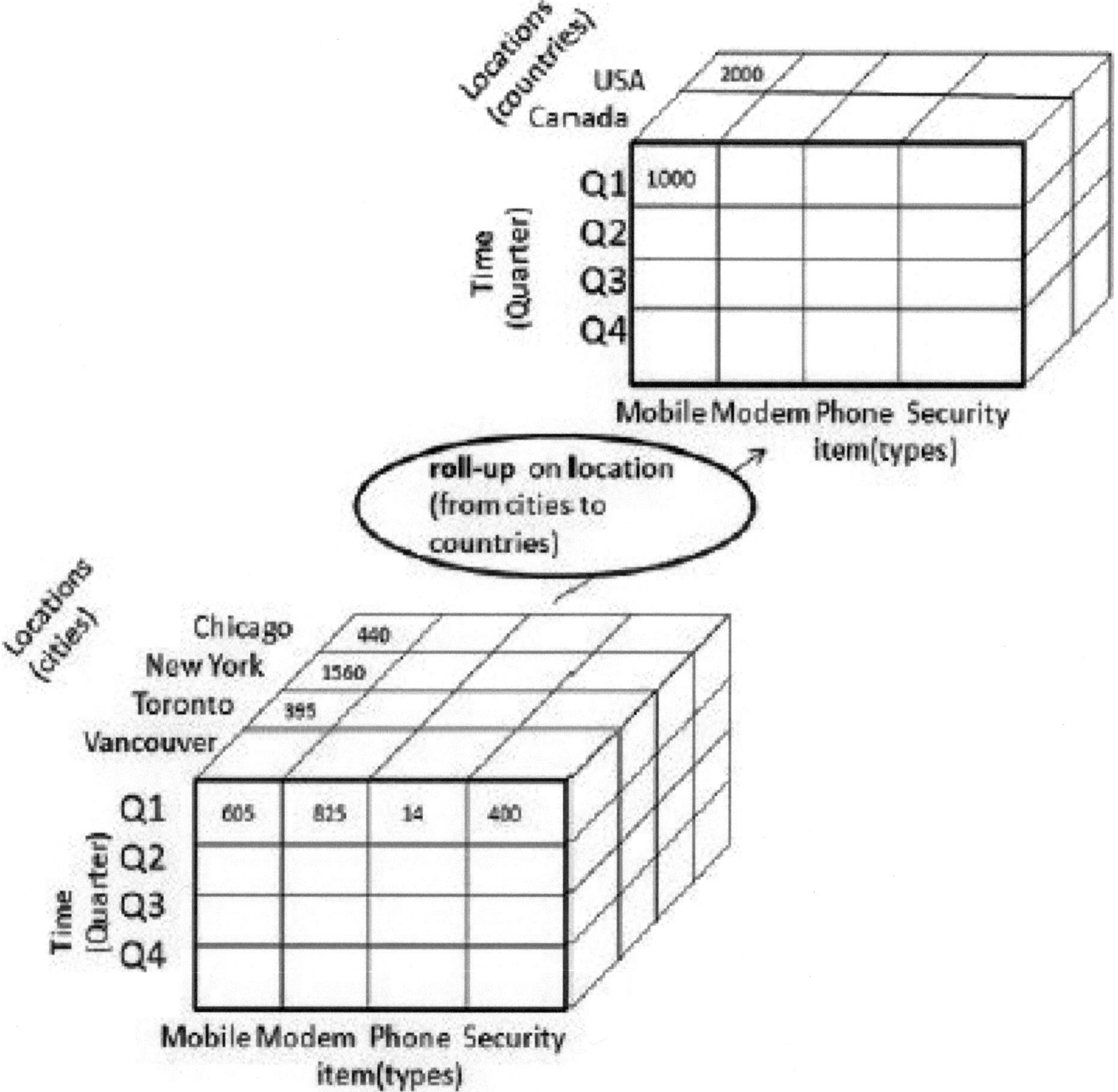

Roll-up is performed by climbing up a concept hierarchy for the dimension location.

Initially the concept hierarchy was "street < city < province < country".

On rolling up, the data is aggregated by ascending the location hierarchy from the level of city to the level of country.

The data is grouped into cities rather than countries.

When roll-up is performed, one or more dimensions from the data cube are removed.

Drill-downDrill-down is the reverse operation of roll-up. It is performed by either of the following ways:

By stepping down a concept hierarchy for a dimension

By introducing a new dimension.

The following diagram illustrates how drill-down works:

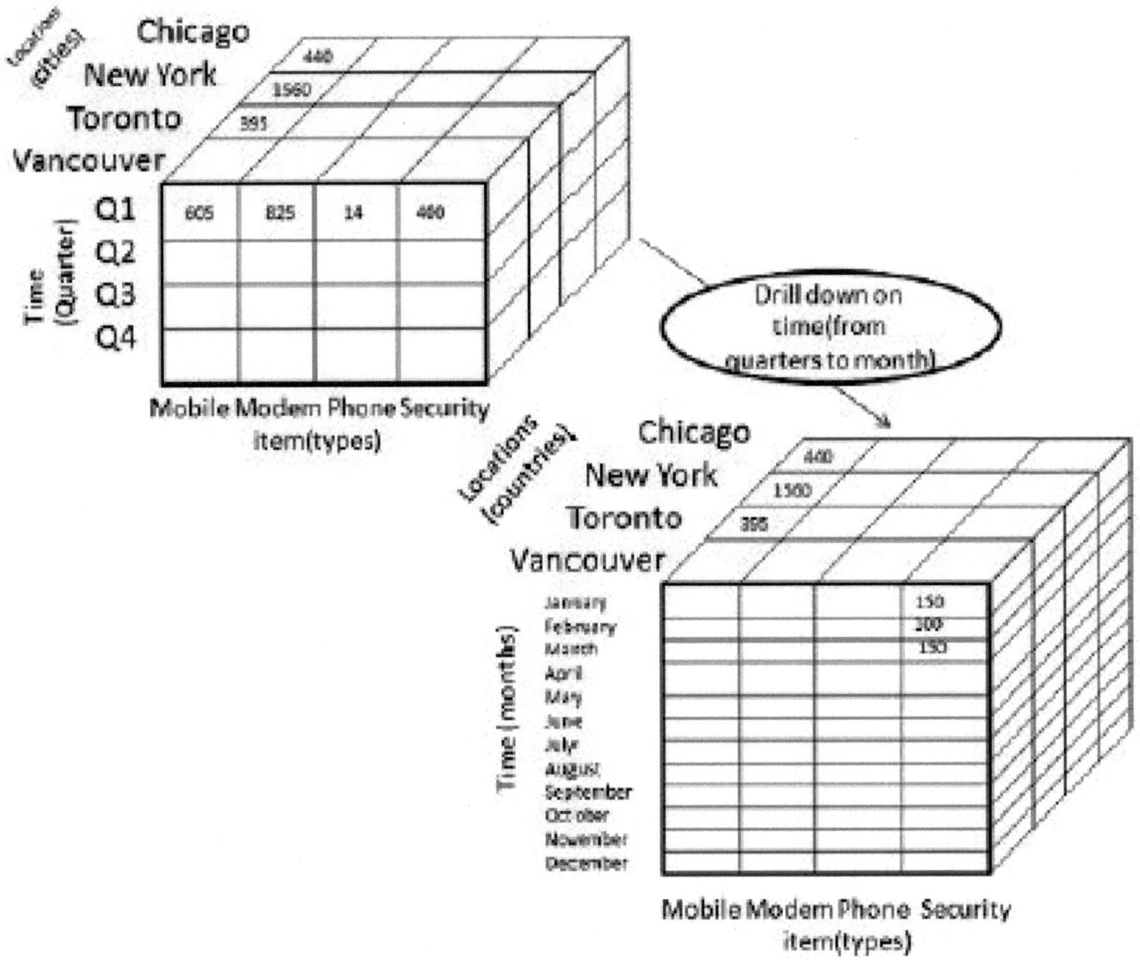

Drill-down is performed by stepping down a concept hierarchy for the dimension time.

Initially the concept hierarchy was "day < month < quarter < year."

On drilling down, the time dimension is descended from the level of quarter to the level of month.

When drill-down is performed, one or more dimensions from the data cube are added.

It navigates the data from less detailed data to highly detailed data.

Slice

The slice operation selects one particular dimension from a given cube and provides a new subcube.

Consider the following diagram that shows how slice works.

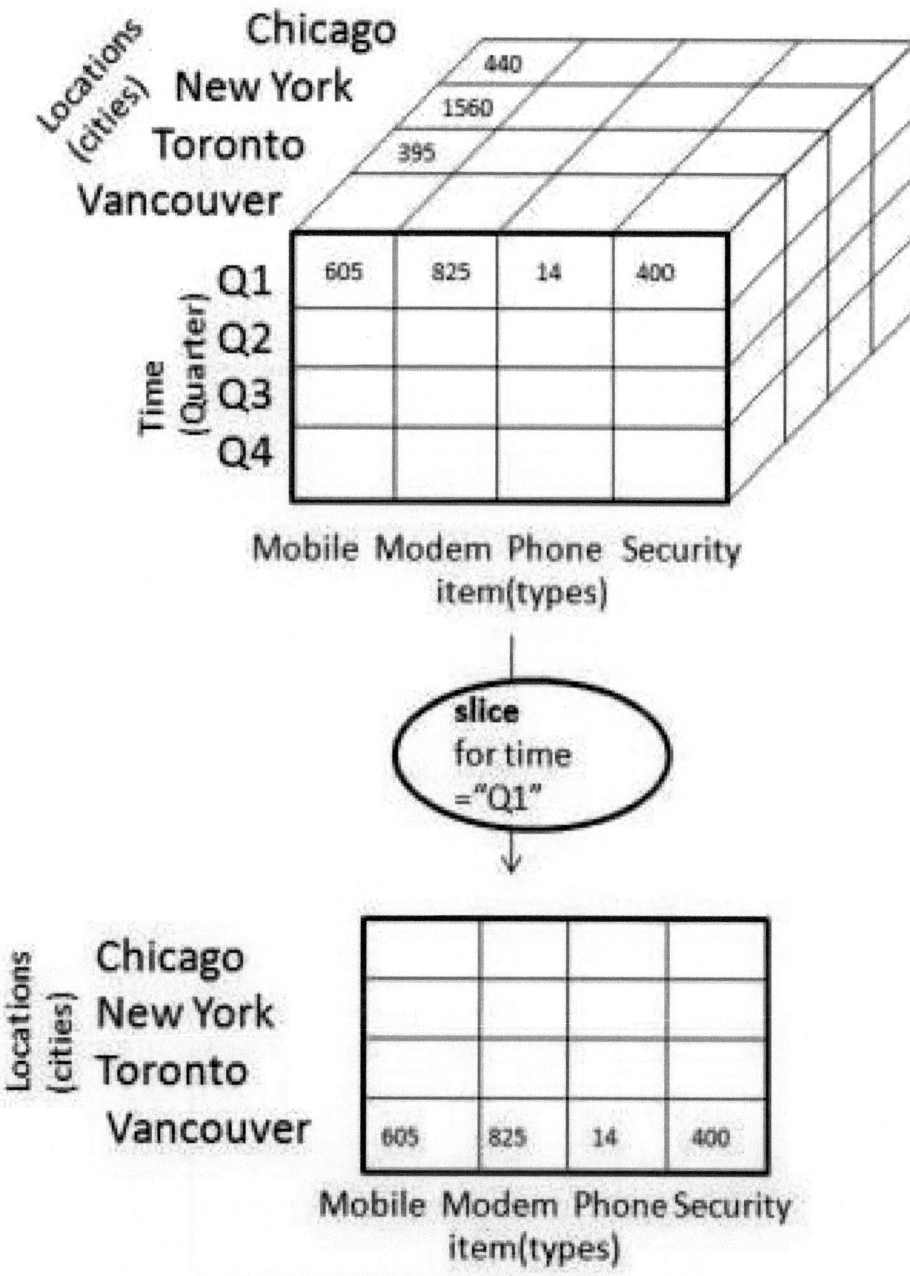

Here Slice is performed for the dimension "time" using the criterion time = "Q1".
It will form a new sub-cube by selecting one or more dimensions.

Dice

Dice selects two or more dimensions from a given cube and provides a new sub-cube.
Consider the following diagram that shows the dice operation.

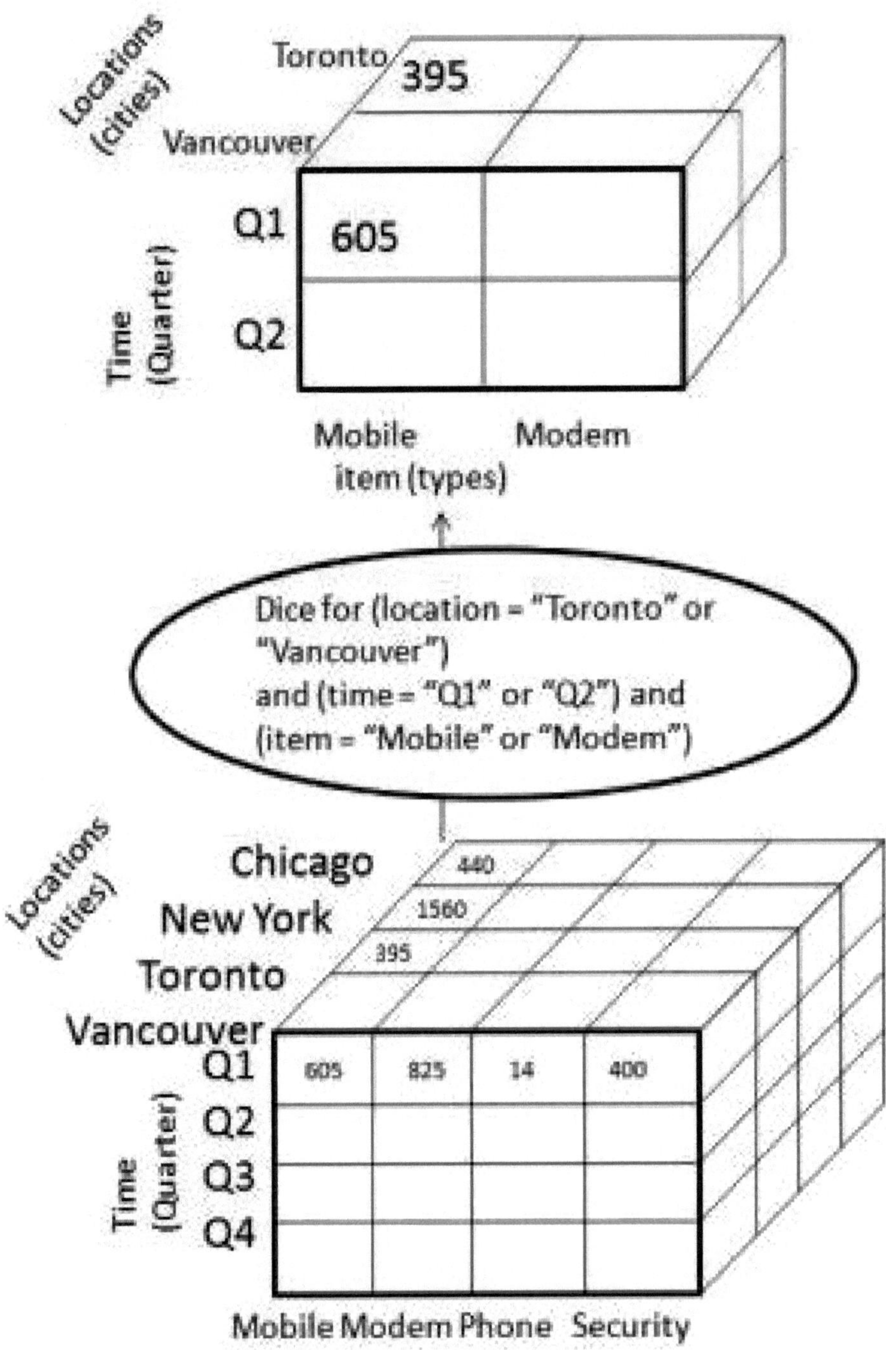

The dice operation on the cube based on the following selection criteria involves three dimensions.
(location = "Toronto" or "Vancouver")
(time = "Q1" or "Q2")
(item =" Mobile" or "Modem")

Pivot

The pivot operation is also known as rotation.
It rotates the data axes in view in order to provide an alternative presentation of data.
Consider the following diagram that shows the pivot operation.

In this the item and location axes in 2-D slice are rotated.

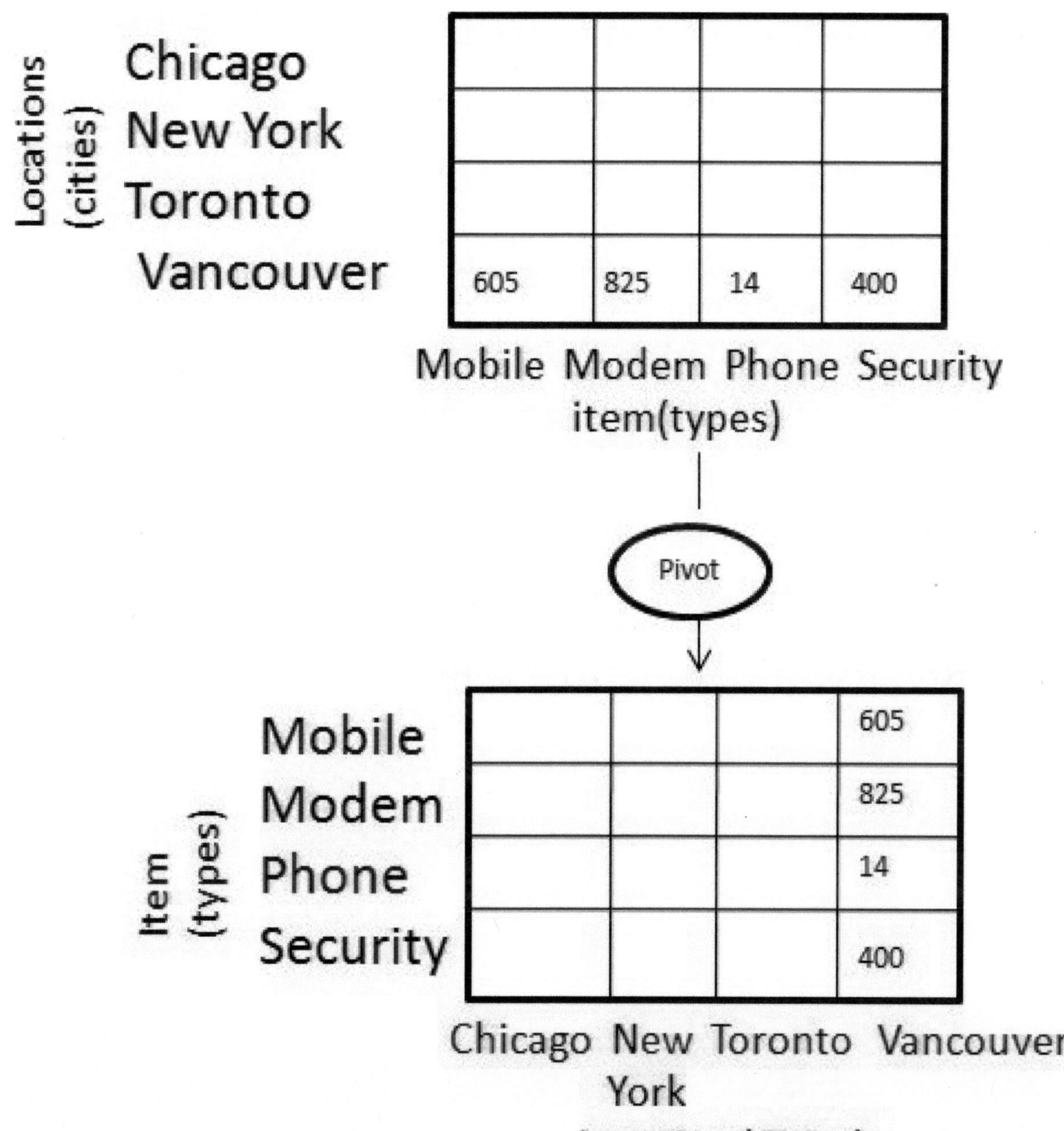

Types of OLAP Servers.

We have four types of OLAP servers:

Relational OLAP

ROLAP servers are placed between relational back-end server and client front-end tools.

To store and manage warehouse data, ROLAP uses relational or extended-relational DBMS.

ROLAP includes the following:

Implementation of aggregation navigation logic.

Optimization for each DBMS back end.

Additional tools and services.

Multidimensional OLAP

MOLAP uses array-based multidimensional storage engines for multidimensional views of data.

With multidimensional data stores, the storage utilization may be low if the data set is sparse.

Many MOLAP server use two levels of data storage representation to handle dense and sparse data sets.

Hybrid OLAP (HOLAP)

Hybrid OLAP is a combination of both ROLAP and MOLAP.

It offers higher scalability of ROLAP and faster computation of MOLAP.

HOLAP servers allows to store the large data volumes of detailed information.

The aggregations are stored separately in MOLAP store.

Specialized SQL Servers

Specialized SQL servers provide advanced query language and query processing support for SQL queries over star and snowflake schemas in a read-only environment.

III

Data Mining and Business Intelligence

"Data Mining". With the help of a suitable diagram explain the process of knowledge discovery from databases.

Data Mining: "It refers to extracting or "mining" knowledge from large amounts of data."

Also refers as Knowledge mining from data.

Many people treat data mining as a synonym for another popularly used term, Knowledge Discovery from Data, or KDD.

Data mining can be viewed as a result of the natural evolution of information technology.

The abundance of data, coupled with the need for powerful data analysis tools, has been described as data rich but information poor situation.

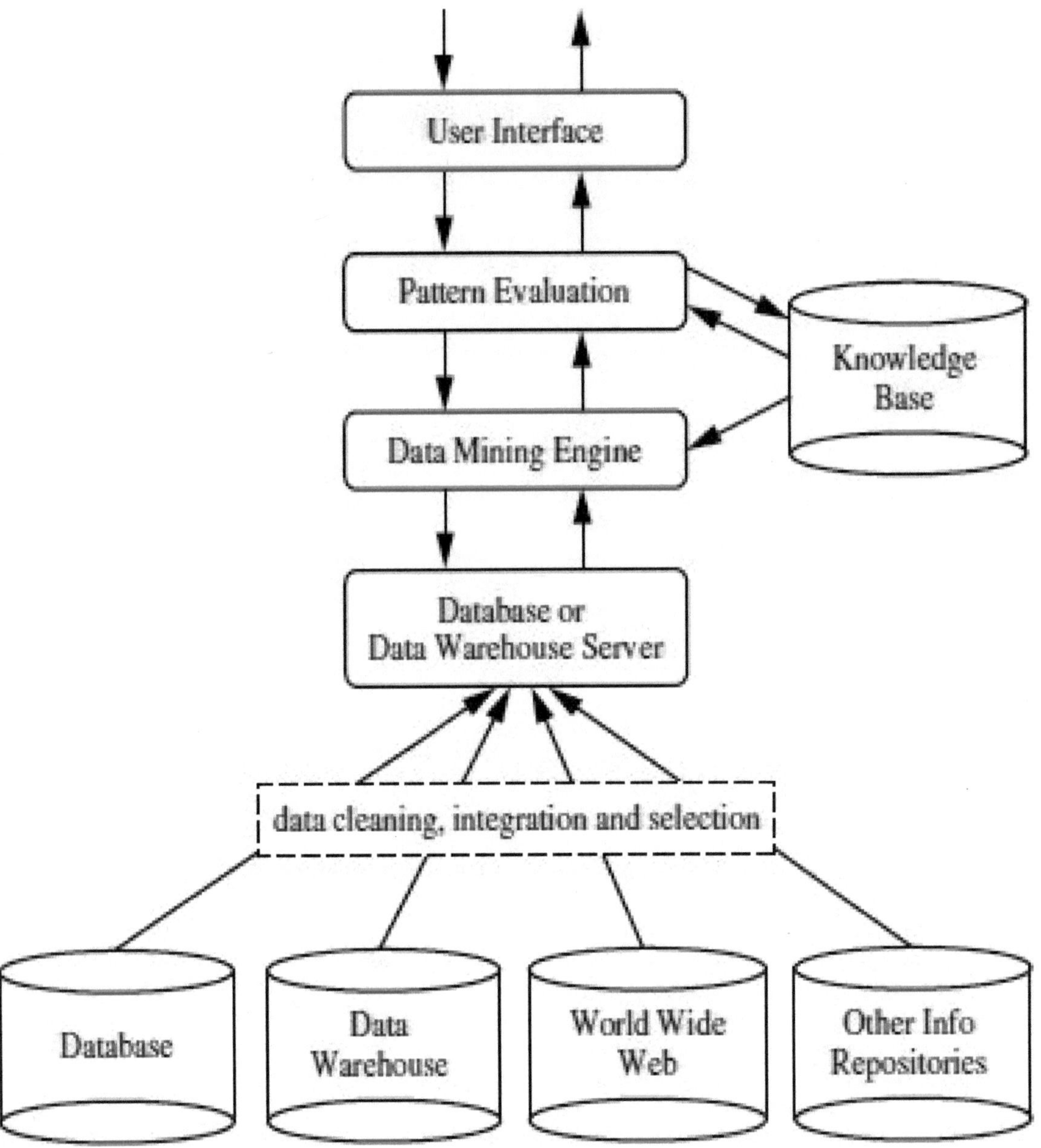

Knowledge base: This is the domain knowledge that is used to guide the search or evaluate the interestingness of resulting patterns. Such knowledge can include concept hierarchies, used to organize attributes or attribute values into different levels of abstraction.

Data warehouses typically provide a simple and concise view around particular subject issues by excluding data that are not useful in the decision support process.

Knowledge such as user beliefs, which can be used to assess a pattern's interestingness based on its unexpectedness, may also be included. Other examples of domain knowledge are additional interestingness constraints or thresholds, and metadata (e.g., describing data from multiple heterogeneous sources).

Data mining engine: This is essential to the data mining system and ideally consists of a set of functional modules for tasks such as characterization, association and correlation analysis, classification, prediction, cluster analysis, outlier analysis, and evolution analysis.

Pattern evaluation module: This component typically employs interestingness measures and interacts with the data mining modules so as to focus the search toward interesting patterns.

It may use interestingness thresholds to filter out discovered patterns. Alternatively, the pattern evaluation module may be integrated with the mining module, depending on the implementation of the data mining method used.

For efficient data mining, it is highly recommended to push the evaluation of pattern interestingness as deep as possible into the mining process so as to confine the search to only the interesting patterns.

KDD (Knowledge Discovery from Data) Process

KDD stands for knowledge discoveries from database. There are some pre-processing operations which are required to make pure data in data warehouse before use that data for Data Mining processes.

A view data mining as simply an essential step in the process of knowledge discovery. Knowledge discovery as a process is depicted in Figure 2 and consists of an iterative sequence of the following steps:

Data cleaning: To remove noise and inconsistent data.

Data integration: where multiple data sources may be combined.

Data selection: where data relevant to the analysis task are retrieved from the database.

Data transformation: where data are transformed or consolidated into forms appropriate for mining by performing summary or aggregation operations, for instance.

Data mining: An essential process where intelligent methods are applied in order to extract data patterns.

Pattern evaluation: To identify the truly interesting patterns representing knowledge based on some interestingness measures.

Knowledge presentation: where visualization and knowledge representation techniques are used to present the mined knowledge to the user.

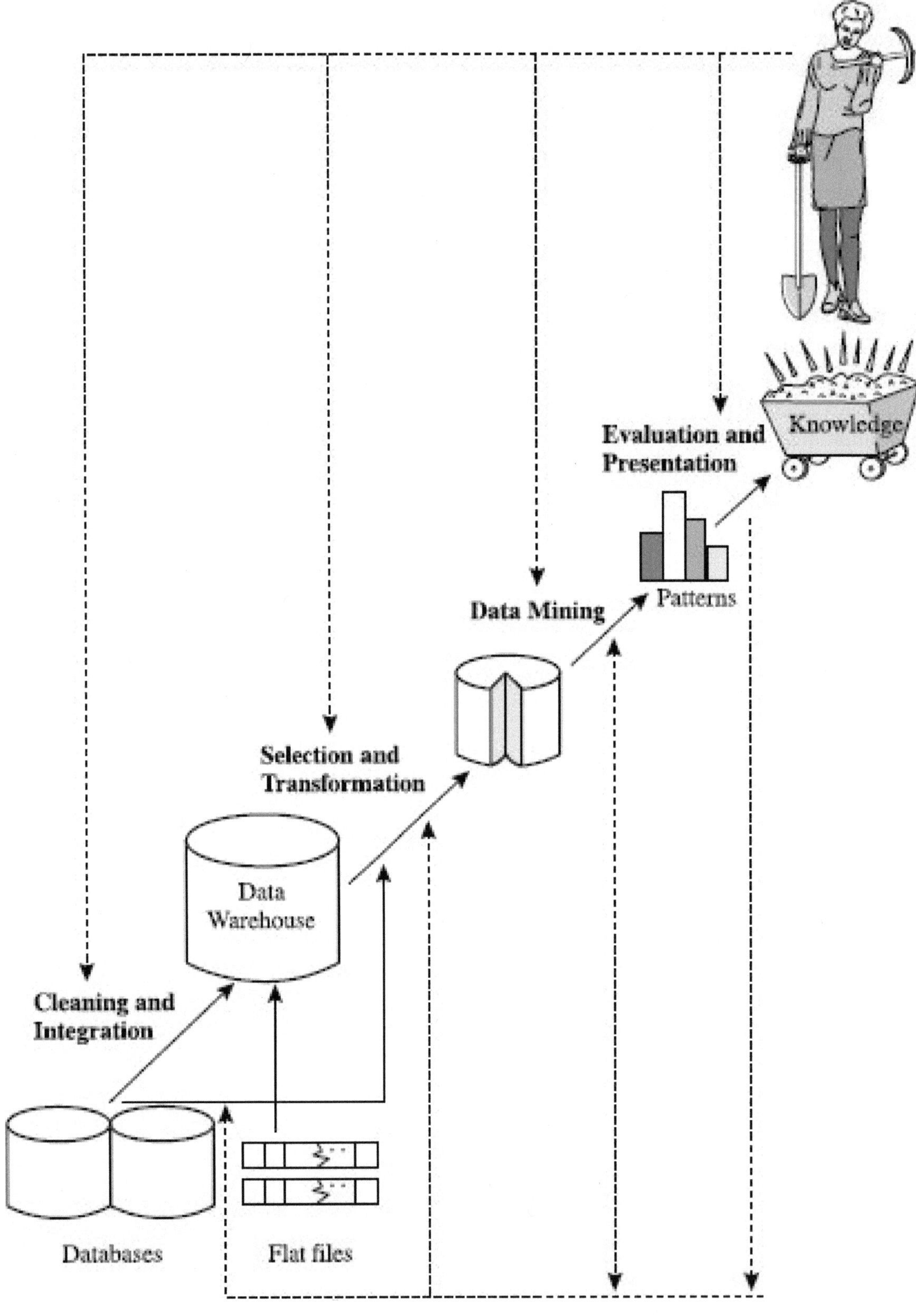

KDD refers to the overall process of discovering useful knowledge from data. It involves the evaluation and possibly interpretation of the patterns to make the decision of what qualifies as knowledge. It also includes the choice of encoding schemes, preprocessing, sampling, and projections of the data prior to the data mining step.

Data mining refers to the application of algorithms for extracting patterns from data without the additional steps of the KDD process.

Objective of Pre-processing on data is to remove noise from data or to remove redundant data.

There are mainly 4 types of Pre-processing Activities included in KDD Process that is shown in fig. as Data cleaning, Data integration, Data transformation, Data reduction.

Major issues in data mining

Data Mining is a dynamic and fast-expanding field with great strengths. Major issues in data mining research, partitioning them into five groups: Mining methodology, User interaction, Efficiency and scalability, Diversity of data types, and Data mining & Society.

Many of these issues have been addressed in recent data mining research and development to a certain extent and are now considered data mining requirements; others are still at the research stage. The issues continue to stimulate further investigation and improvement in data mining.

Mining Methodology: This involves the investigation of new kinds of knowledge, mining in multidimensional space, integrating methods from other disciplines, and the consideration of semantic ties among data objects.

In addition, mining methodologies should consider issues such as data uncertainty, noise, and incompleteness.

Mining various and new kinds of knowledge: Data mining covers a wide spectrum of data analysis and knowledge discovery tasks, from data characterization and discrimination to association and correlation analysis, classification, regression, clustering, outlier analysis, sequence analysis, and trend and evolution analysis.

These tasks may use the same database in different ways and require the development of numerous data mining techniques. Due to the diversity of applications, new mining tasks continue to emerge, making data mining a dynamic and fast-growing field.

For example, for effective knowledge discovery in information networks, integrated clustering and ranking may lead to the discovery of high-quality clusters and object ranks in large networks.

Mining knowledge in multidimensional space: When searching for knowledge in large data sets, we can explore the data in multidimensional space. That is, we can search for interesting patterns among combinations of dimensions (attributes) at varying levels of abstraction. Such mining is known as (exploratory) multidimensional data mining.

In many cases, data can be aggregated or viewed as a multidimensional data cube. Mining

knowledge in cube space can substantially enhance the power and flexibility of data mining.

Data mining—an interdisciplinary effort: The power of data mining can be substantially enhanced by integrating new methods from multiple disciplines. For example, to mine data with natural language text, it makes sense to fuse data mining methods with methods of information retrieval and natural language processing.

As another example, consider the mining of software bugs in large programs. This form of mining, known as bug mining, benefits from the incorporation of software engineering knowledge into the data mining process.

Handling uncertainty, noise, or incompleteness of data: Data often contain noise, errors, exceptions, or uncertainty, or are incomplete. Errors and noise may confuse the data mining process, leading to the derivation of erroneous patterns.

Data cleaning, data preprocessing, outlier detection and removal, and uncertainty reasoning are examples of techniques that need to be integrated with the data mining process.

User Interaction: The user plays an important role in the data mining process. Interesting areas of research include how to interact with a data mining system, how to incorporate a user's background knowledge in mining, and how to visualize and comprehend data mining results.

Interactive mining: The data mining process should be highly interactive. Thus, it is important to build flexible user interfaces and an exploratory mining environment, facilitating the user's interaction with the system.

A user may like to first sample a set of data, explore general characteristics of the data, and estimate potential mining results. Interactive mining should allow users to dynamically change the focus of a search, to refine mining requests based on returned results, and to drill, dice, and pivot through the data and knowledge space interactively, dynamically exploring "cube space" while mining.

Incorporation of background knowledge: Background knowledge, constraints, rules, and other information regarding the domain under study should be incorporated into the knowledge discovery process. Such knowledge can be used for pattern evaluation as well as to guide the search toward interesting patterns.

Presentation and visualization of data mining results: How can a data mining system present data mining results, vividly and flexibly, so that the discovered knowledge can be easily understood and directly usable by humans? This is especially crucial if the data mining process is interactive.

It requires the system to adopt expressive knowledge representations, user-friendly interfaces, and visualization techniques.

Efficiency and Scalability: Efficiency and scalability are always considered when comparing data mining algorithms. As data amounts continue to multiply, these two factors are especially critical.

Efficiency and scalability of data mining algorithms: Data mining algorithms must be efficient and scalable in order to effectively extract information from huge amounts of data in many data repositories or in dynamic data streams.

In other words, the running time of a data mining algorithm must be predictable, short, and acceptable by applications. Efficiency, scalability, performance, optimization, and the ability to execute in real time are key criteria that drive the development of many new data mining algorithms.

Parallel, distributed, and incremental mining algorithms: The humongous size of many data sets, the wide distribution of data, and the computational complexity of some data mining methods are factors that motivate the development of parallel and distributed data- intensive mining algorithms. Such algorithms first partition the data into "pieces."

Each piece is processed, in parallel, by searching for patterns. The parallel processes may interact with one another. The patterns from each partition are eventually merged.

Diversity of Database Types: The wide diversity of database types brings about challenges to data mining. These includes are as below.

Handling complex types of data: Diverse applications generate a wide spectrum of new data types, from structured data such as relational and data warehouse data to semi- structured and unstructured data; from stable data repositories to dynamic data streams; from simple data objects to temporal data, biological sequences, sensor data, spatial data, hypertext data, multimedia data, software program code, Web data, and social network data.

It is unrealistic to expect one data mining system to mine all kinds of data, given the diversity of data types and the different goals of data mining. Domain- or application-dedicated data mining systems are being constructed for in depth mining of specific kinds of data.

The construction of effective and efficient data mining tools for diverse applications remains a challenging and active area of research.

Mining dynamic, networked, and global data repositories: Multiple sources of data are connected by the Internet and various kinds of networks, forming gigantic, distributed, and heterogeneous global information systems and networks.

The discovery of knowledge from different sources of structured, semi-structured, or unstructured yet interconnected data with diverse data semantics poses great challenges to data mining.

Data Mining and Society: How does data mining impact society? What steps can data mining take to preserve the privacy of individuals? Do we use data mining in our daily lives without even knowing that we do? These questions raise the following issues:

Social impacts of data mining: With data mining penetrating our everyday lives, it is important to study the impact of data mining on society. How can we used at a mining technology to benefit society? How can we guard against its misuse?

The improper disclosure or use of data and the potential violation of individual privacy and data protection rights are areas of concern that need to be addressed.

Privacy-preserving data mining: Data mining will help scientific discovery, business management, economy recovery, and security protection (e.g., the real-time discovery of intruders and cyberattacks).

However, it poses the risk of disclosing an individual's personal information. Studies on privacy-preserving data publishing and data mining are ongoing. The philosophy is to observe data sensitivity and preserve people's privacy while performing successful data mining.

Invisible data mining: We cannot expect everyone in society to learn and master data mining techniques. More and more systems should have data mining functions built within so that people can perform data mining or use data mining results simply by mouse clicking, without any knowledge of data mining algorithms.

Intelligent search engines and Internet-based stores perform such invisible data mining by incorporating data mining into their components to improve their functionality and performance. This is done often unbeknownst to the user.

For example, when purchasing items online, users may be unaware that the store is likely collecting data on the buying patterns of its customers, which may be used to recommend other items for purchase in the future.

Types of data on which mining can be performed

Data mining can be applied to any kind of data as long as the data are meaningful for a target application. The most basic forms of data for mining applications are database data, data warehouse data, and transactional data.

Data mining can also be applied to other forms of data (e.g., data streams, ordered/sequence data, graph or networked data, spatial data, text data, multimedia data, and the WWW).

Database Data: A database system, also called a database management system (DBMS), consists of a collection of interrelated data, known as a database, and a set of software programs to manage and access the data.

The software programs provide mechanisms for defining database structures and data storage; for specifying and managing concurrent, shared, or distributed data access; and for ensuring consistency and security of the information stored despite system crashes or attempts at unauthorized access.

A relational database is a collection of tables, each of which is assigned a unique name. Each table consists of a set of attributes (columns or fields) and usually stores a large set of tuples (records or rows).

Each tuple in a relational table represents an object identified by a unique key and described by a set of attribute values. A semantic data model, such as an entity-relationship (ER) data model, is often constructed for relational databases.

Example

A relational database for AllElectronics. The company is described by the following relation tables: customer, item, employee, and branch.

The relation customer consists of a set of attributes describing the customer information, including a unique customer identity number (cust_ID), customer name, address, age, occupation, annual income, credit information, and category.

Similarly, each of the relations item, employee, and branch consists of a set of attributes describing the properties of these entities. Tables can also be used to represent the relationships between or among multiple entities.

In our example, these include purchases (customer purchases items, creating a sales transaction handled by an employee), items sold (lists items sold in a given transaction), and works at (employee works at a branch of AllElectronics).

Customer (cust_ID, name, address, age, occupation, annual income, credit information, category, ...)

Item (item ID, brand, category, type, price, place made, supplier, cost, ...)

employee (empl_ID, name, category, group, salary, commission, ...)

Branch (branch ID, name, address, ...)

Purchases (trans ID, cust_ID, empl_ID, date, time, method paid, amount)

Items sold (trans ID, item ID, Qty)

Works at (empl_ID, branch_ID)

Relational data can be accessed by database queries written in a relational query language (e.g., SQL) or with the assistance of graphical user interfaces.

A given query is transformed into a set of relational operations, such as join, selection, and projection, and is then optimized for efficient processing. A query allows retrieval of specified subsets of the data. Suppose that your job is to analyze the AllElectronics data.

Through the use of relational queries, you can ask things like, "Show me a list of all items that were sold in the last quarter." Relational languages also use aggregate functions such as sum, avg (average), count, max (maximum), and min (minimum). Using aggregates allows you to ask: "Show me the total sales of the last month, grouped by branch," or "How many sales transactions occurred in the month of December?" or "Which salesperson had the highest sales?"

Data Warehouse Data: Suppose that AllElectronics is a successful international company with branches around the world. Each branch has its own set of databases. The president of AllElectronics has asked you to provide an analysis of the company's sales per item type per branch for the third quarter.

This is a difficult task, particularly since the relevant data are spread out over several databases

physically located at numerous sites.

If AllElectronics had a data warehouse, this task would be easy. "A data warehouse is a repository of information collected from multiple sources, stored under a unified schema, and usually residing at a single site."

Data warehouses are constructed via a process of data cleaning, data integration, data transformation, data loading, and periodic data refreshing.

To facilitate decision making, the data in a data warehouse are organized around major subjects (e.g., customer, item, supplier, and activity). The data are stored to provide information from a historical perspective, such as in the past 6 to 12 months, and are typically summarized.

For example, rather than storing the details of each sales transaction, the data warehouse may store a summary of the transactions per item type for each store or, summarized to a higher level, for each sales region.

A data warehouse is usually modeled by a multidimensional data structure, called a data cube, in which each dimension corresponds to an attribute or a set of attributes in the schema, and each cell stores the value of some aggregate measure such as count or sum (sales amount). A data cube provides a multidimensional view of data and allows the precomputation and fast access of summarized data.

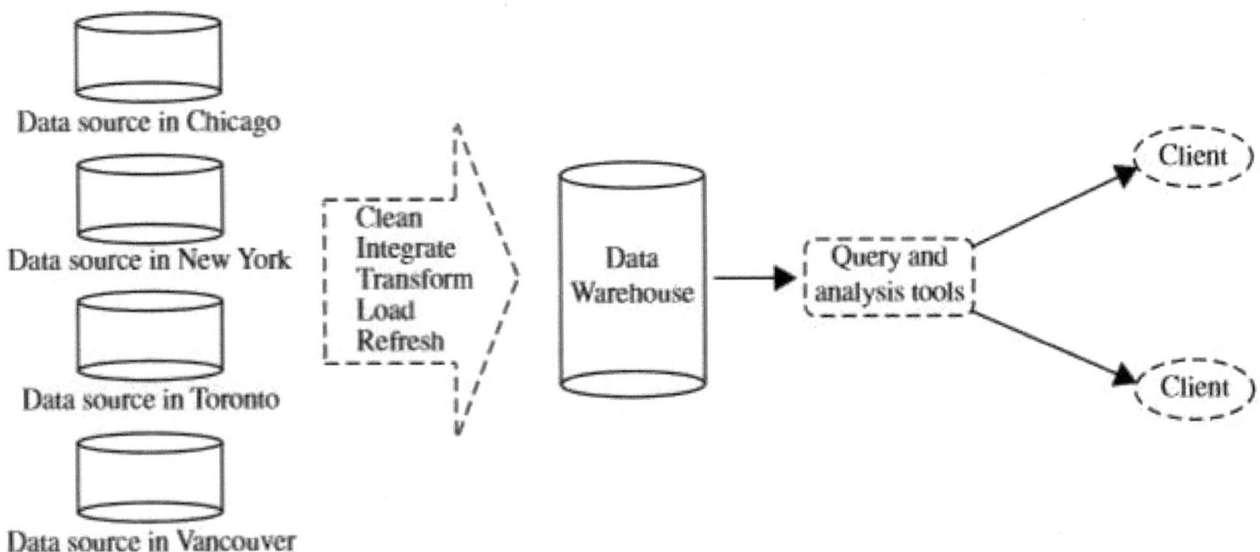

Although data warehouse tools help support data analysis, additional tools for data mining are often needed for in-depth analysis. Multidimensional data mining (also called exploratory multidimensional data mining) performs data mining in multidimensional space in an OLAP style.

That is, it allows the exploration of multiple combinations of dimensions at varying levels of granularity in data mining, and thus has greater potential for discovering interesting patterns representing knowledge.

Transactional Data: In general, each record in a transactional database captures a transaction, such as a customer's purchase, a flight booking, or a user's clicks on a web page. A transaction typically includes a unique transaction identity number (trans_ID) and a list of the items making up the transaction, such as the items purchased in the transaction.

A transactional database may have additional tables, which contain other information related to the transactions, such as item description, information about the salesperson or the branch, and so on.

Example

A transactional database for AllElectronics.

Transactions can be stored in a table, with one record per transaction. A fragment of a transactional database for AllElectronics is shown in Figure 4. From the relational database point of view, the sales table in the figure is a nested relation because the attribute list of item IDs contains a set of items.

Because most relational database systems do not support nested relational structures, the transactional database is usually either stored in a flat file in a format similar to the table in Figure .

As an analyst of AllElectronics, you may ask, "Which items sold well together?" This kind of market basket data analysis would enable you to bundle groups of items together as a strategy for boosting sales.

For example, given the knowledge that printers are commonly purchased together with computers, you could offer certain printers at a steep discount (or even for free) to customers buying selected computers, in the hopes of selling more computers (which are often more expensive than printers).

A traditional database system is not able to perform market basket data analysis. Fortunately, data mining on transactional data can do so by mining frequent item sets, that is, sets of items that are frequently sold together.

Trans_ID	List of item IDs
T100	I1, I3, I8, I16
T200	I2, I8
...	...

IV

Data Preprocessing

Data Preprocessing is needed and which are the techniques used for data Preprocessing

Today's real-world databases are highly susceptible to noisy, missing, and inconsistent data due to their typically huge size (often several gigabytes or more) and their likely origin from multiple, heterogeneous sources.

Low-quality data will lead to low-quality mining results. How can the data be preprocessed in order to help improve the quality of the data and, consequently, of the mining results? How can the data be preprocessed so as to improve the efficiency and ease of the mining process?

Data have quality if they satisfy the requirements of the intended use. There are many factors comprising data quality, including accuracy, completeness, consistency, timeliness, believability, and interpretability.

Example

Imagine that you are a manager at AllElectronics and have been charged with analyzing the company's data with respect to your branch's sales.

You immediately set out to perform this task. You carefully inspect the company's database and data warehouse, identifying and selecting the attributes or dimensions (e.g., item, price, and units sold) to be included in your analysis.

Alas! You notice that several of the attributes for various tuples have no recorded value. For your analysis, you would like to include information as to whether each item purchased was advertised as on sale, yet you discover that this information has not been recorded.

Furthermore, users of your database system have reported errors, unusual values, and inconsistencies in the data recorded for some transactions.

In other words, the data you wish to analyze by data mining techniques are incomplete (lacking attribute values or certain attributes of interest, or containing only aggregate data); inaccurate or noisy (containing errors, or values that deviate from the expected); and inconsistent (e.g., containing discrepancies in the department codes used to categorize items).

Above example illustrates three of the elements defining data quality: accuracy, completeness, and consistency.

Inaccurate, incomplete, and inconsistent data are commonplace properties of large real-world databases and data warehouses.

There are many possible reasons for inaccurate data (i.e., having incorrect attribute values). The data collection instruments used may be faulty.

There may have been human or computer errors occurring at data entry. Users may purposely submit incorrect data values for mandatory fields when they do not wish to submit personal information (e.g., by choosing the default value "January 1" displayed for birthday). This is known as disguised missing data. Errors in data transmission can also occur.

There may be technology limitations such as limited buffer size for coordinating synchronized data transfer and consumption. Incorrect data may also result from inconsistencies in naming conventions or data codes, or inconsistent formats for input fields (e.g., date).

Incomplete data can occur for a number of reasons. Attributes of interest may not always be available, such as customer information for sales transaction data.

Other data may not be included simply because they were not considered important at the time of entry. Relevant data may not be recorded due to a misunderstanding or because of equipment malfunctions. Data that were inconsistent with other recorded data may have been deleted.

Furthermore, the recording of the data history or modifications may have been overlooked. Missing data, particularly for tuples with missing values for some attributes, may need to be inferred.

Data Preprocessing Methods/Techniques:

Data Cleaning routines work to "clean" the data by filling in missing values, smoothing noisy data, identifying or removing outliers, and resolving inconsistencies.

Data Integration which combines data from multiple sources into a coherent data store, as in data warehousing.

Data Transformation, the data are transformed or consolidated into forms appropriate for mining

Data Reduction obtains a reduced representation of the data set that is much smaller in volume, yet produces the same (or almost the same) analytical results.

Explain Mean, Median, Mode, Variance & Standard Deviation in brief.

Mean: The sample mean is the average and is computed as the sum of all the observed outcomes from the sample divided by the total number of events. We use x as the symbol for the sample mean. In math terms,

$$\bar{x} = \frac{1}{n} \sum_{i=1}^{n} x$$

where n is the sample size and the x correspond to the observed valued.

Let's look to Find out Mean.

Suppose you randomly sampled six acres in the Desolation Wilderness for a non-indigenous weed and came up with the following counts of this weed in this region: 34, 43, 81, 106, 106 and 115

We compute the sample mean by adding and dividing by the number of samples, 6. 34 + 43 + 81 + 106 + 106 + 115

We can say that the sample mean of non-indigenous weed is 80.83.

The mode of a set of data is the number with the highest frequency. In the above example 106 is the mode, since it occurs twice and the rest of the outcomes occur only once.

The population mean is the average of the entire population and is usually impossible to compute. We use the Greek letter μ for the population mean.

Median: One problem with using the mean, is that it often does not depict the typical outcome. If there is one outcome that is very far from the rest of the data, then the mean will be strongly affected by this outcome. Such an outcome is called and outlier.

An alternative measure is the median; the median is the middle score. If we have an even number of events, we take the average of the two middles. The median is better for describing the typical value. It is often used for income and home prices.

Let's Look to Find out Median.

Suppose you randomly selected 10 house prices in the South Lake area. You are interested in the typical house price. In $100,000 the prices were: 2.7, 2.9, 3.1, 3.4, 3.7, 4.1, 4.3, 4.7, 4.7, 40.8.

If we computed the mean, we would say that the average house price is 744,000. Although this number is true, it does not reflect the price for available housing in South Lake Tahoe.

A closer look at the data shows that the house valued at 40.8 x $100,000 = $4.08 million skews the data. Instead, we use the median. Since there is an even number of outcomes, we take the average of the middle two is 3.9.

3.7 + 4.1
= 3.9
2

The median house price is $390,000. This better reflects what house shoppers should expect to spend.

Mode: The mode is another measure of central tendency. The mode for a set of data is the value that occurs most frequently in the set.

Therefore, it can be determined for qualitative and quantitative attributes. It is possible for the greatest frequency to correspond to several different values, which results in more than one mode. Data sets with one, two, or three modes are respectively called unimodal, bimodal, and trimodal.

In general, a dataset with two or more modes is multimodal. At the other extreme, if each data value occurs only once, then there is no mode.

Let's Look for find Mode.

In Above Example We Consider 4.7 As Mode.

Variance & Standard Deviation: The mean, mode and median do a nice job in telling where the center of the data set is, but often we are interested in more.

For example, a pharmaceutical engineer develops a new drug that regulates iron in the blood. Suppose she finds out that the average sugar content after taking the medication is the optimal level. This does not mean that the drug is effective. There is a possibility that half of the patients have dangerously low sugar content while the other half have dangerously high content.

Instead of the drug being an effective regulator, it is a deadly poison. What the pharmacist needs is a measure of how far the data is spread apart. This is what the variance and standard deviation do. First we show the formulas for these measurements. Then we will go through the steps on how to use the formulas.

We define the variance to be

$$s^2 = \frac{1}{n-1}\sum_{i=1}^{n}(x-\bar{x})^2$$

- and the standard deviation to be

$$s = \sqrt{\frac{1}{n-1}\sum_{i=1}^{n}(x-\bar{x})^2}$$

Variance and Standard Deviation: Step by Step

Calculate the mean, x.

Write a table that subtracts the mean from each observed value.

Square each of the differences.

Add this column.

Divide by n -1 where n is the number of items in the sample this is the variance.

To get the standard deviation we take the square root of the variance.

Let's Look to Find out variance & standard deviation.

The owner of the Indian restaurant is interested in how much people spend at the restaurant. He examines 10 randomly selected receipts for parties of four and writes down the following data.

44, 50, 38, 96, 42, 47, 40, 39, 46, 50

He calculated the mean by adding and dividing by 10 to get Average(Mean) = 49.2.

Below is the table for getting the standard deviation:

x	x - 49.2	$(x - 49.2)^2$
44	-5.2	27.04
50	0.8	0.64
38	11.2	125.44
96	46.8	2190.24
42	-7.2	51.84
47	-2.2	4.84
40	-9.2	84.64
39	-10.2	104.04
46	-3.2	10.24
50	0.8	0.64
Total		2600.4

Now 2600.4/10 – 1 = 288.7

Hence the variance is 289 and the standard deviation is the square root of 289 = 17.

Since the standard deviation can be thought of measuring how far the data values lie from the mean, we take the mean and move one standard deviation in either direction. The mean for this example was about 49.2 and the standard deviation was 17.

We have: 49.2 - 17 = 32.2 and 49.2 + 17 = 66.2

What this means is that most of the patrons probably spend between $32.20 and $66.20.

The sample standard deviation will be denoted by s and the population standard deviation will be denoted by the Greek letter σ.

The sample variance will be denoted by s2 and the population variance will be denoted by σ2.

The variance and standard deviation describe how spread out the data is. If the data all lies close to the mean, then the standard deviation will be small, while if the data is spread out over a large range of values, s will be large. Having outliers will increase the standard deviation.

What is Data Cleaning?

Real-world data tend to be incomplete, noisy, and inconsistent. Data cleaning (or data cleansing) routines attempt to fill in missing values, smooth out noise while identifying outliers, and correct inconsistencies in the data.

Missing Values: Imagine that you need to analyze AllElectronics sales and customer data. You note that many tuples have no recorded value for several attributes such as customer income. How can you go about filling in the missing values for this attribute? Let's look at the following methods.

Ignore the tuple: This is usually done when the class label is missing (assuming the mining task involves classification). This method is not very effective, unless the tuple contains several attributes with missing values. It is especially poor when the percentage of missing values per attribute varies considerably.

By ignoring the tuple, we do not make use of the remaining attributes values in the tuple. Such data could have been useful to the task at hand.

Fill in the missing value manually: In general, this approach is time consuming and may not be feasible given a large data set with many missing values.

Use a global constant to fill in the missing value: Replace all missing attribute values by the same constant such as a label like "Unknown" or 1. If missing values are replaced by, say, "Unknown," then the mining program may mistakenly think that they form an interesting concept, since they all have a value in common—that of "Unknown." Hence, although this method is simple, it is not foolproof.

Use a measure of central tendency for the attribute (e.g., the mean or median) to fill in the missing value: For normal (symmetric) data distributions, the mean can be used, while skewed data distribution should employ the median.

For example, suppose that the data distribution regarding the income of AllElectronics customers is symmetric and that the mean income is $56,000. Use this value to replace the missing value for income.

Use the attribute mean or median for all samples belonging to the same class as the given tuple: For example, if classifying customers according to credit risk, we may replace the missing value with the mean income value for customers in the same credit risk category as

Use the most probable value to fill in the missing value: This may be determined with regression, inference-based tools using a Bayesian formalism, or decision tree induction. For example, using the other customer attributes in your data set, you may construct a decision tree to predict the missing values for income.

Noisy Data: Noise is a random error or variance in a measured variable. Given a numeric attribute such as say, price, how can we "smooth" out the data to remove the noise? Let's look at the following data smoothing techniques.

Binning: Binning methods smooth a sorted data value by consulting its "neighborhood," that is, the values around it. The sorted values are distributed into a number of "buckets," or bins. Because binning methods consult the neighborhood of values, they perform local smoothing.

Figure 1 illustrates some binning techniques. In this example, the data for price are first sorted and then partitioned into equal-frequency bins of size 3 (i.e., each bin contains three values).

In smoothing by bin means, each value in a bin is replaced by the mean value of the bin.

For example, the mean of the values 4, 8, and 15 in Bin 1 is 9. Therefore, each original value in this bin is replaced by the value 9. Similarly, smoothing by bin medians can be employed, in which each bin value is replaced by the bin median. In smoothing by bin boundaries, the minimum and maximum values in a given bin are identified as the bin boundaries. Each bin value is then replaced by the closest boundary value. In general, the larger the width, the greater the effect of the smoothing. Alternatively, bins may be equal width, where the interval range of values in each bin is constant.

Sorted data for price (in dollars): 4, 8, 15, 21, 21, 24, 25, 28, 34

Partition into (equal-frequency) bins:

Bin 1: 4, 8, 15
Bin 2: 21, 21, 24
Bin 3: 25, 28, 34

Smoothing by bin means:

Bin 1: 9, 9, 9
Bin 2: 22, 22, 22
Bin 3: 29, 29, 29

Smoothing by bin boundaries:

Bin 1: 4, 4, 15
Bin 2: 21, 21, 24
Bin 3: 25, 25, 34

that of the given tuple. If the data distribution for a given class is skewed, the median value is a better choice.

Regression: Data smoothing can also be done by regression, a technique that conforms data values to a function. Linear regression involves finding the "best" line to fit two attributes (or variables) so that one attribute can be used to predict the other.

Multiple linear regression is an extension of linear regression, where more than two attributes are involved and the data are fit to a multidimensional surface.

Outlier analysis: Outliers may be detected by clustering, for example, where similar values are organized into groups, or "clusters." Intuitively, values that fall outside of the set of clusters may be considered outliers.

Data Transformation Strategies in data mining

In data transformation, the data are transformed or consolidation to forms appropriate for mining. Strategies for data transformation include the following:

Smoothing, which works to remove noise from the data. Techniques include binning, regression, and clustering.

Attribute construction (or feature construction), where new attributes are constructed and added from the given set of attributes to help the mining process.

Aggregation, where summary or aggregation operations are applied to the data. For example, the daily sales data may be aggregated so as to compute monthly and annual total amounts. This step is typically used in constructing a data cube for data analysis at multiple abstraction levels.

Normalization, where the attribute data are scaled so as to fall within a smaller range, such as–1.0

Discretization, where the raw values of a numeric attribute (e.g. Age) are replaced by interval labels (e.g., 0–10, 11–20, etc.) or conceptual labels (e.g., youth, adult, senior). The labels, in turn, can be recursively organized into higher-level concepts, resulting in a concept hierarchy for the numeric attribute. Figure 2 shows a concept hierarchy for the attribute price. More than one concept hierarchy can be defined for the same attribute to accommodate the needs of various users.

A concept hierarchy for the attribute price, where an interval ($X... $Y] denotes the range from $X (exclusive) to $Y (inclusive). to 1.0, or 0.0 to 1.0.

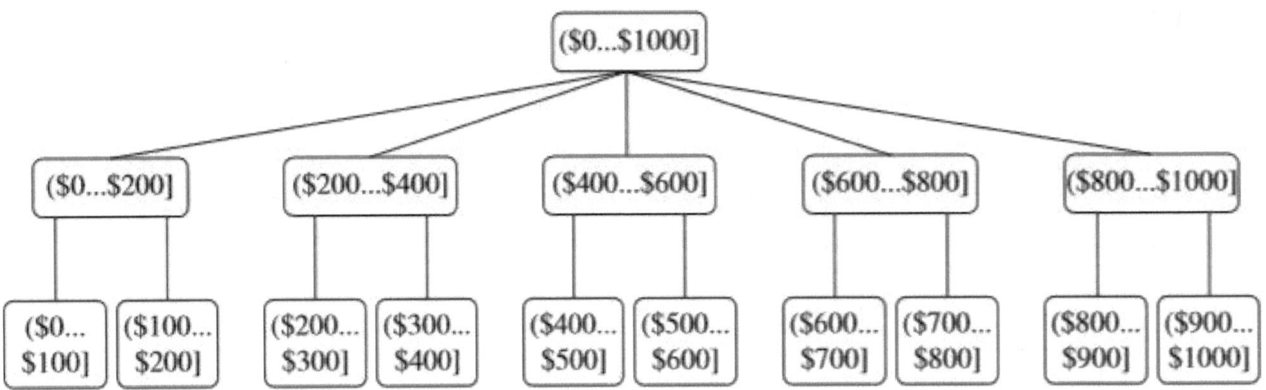

Concept hierarchy generation for nominal data, where attributes such as street can be generalized to higher-level concepts, like city or country. Many hierarchies for nominal attributes are implicit within the database schema and can be automatically defined at the schema definition level.

Data Reduction

Data reduction techniques can be applied to obtain a reduced representation of the data set that is much smaller in volume, yet closely maintains the integrity of the original data. That is, mining on the reduced data set should be more efficient yet produce the analytical results.

Strategies for data reduction include the following:

Data cube aggregation, where aggregation operations are applied to the data in the construction of a data cube.

Attribute subset selection: where irrelevant, weakly relevant, or redundant attributes or dimensions may be detected and removed.

Dimensionality reduction: where encoding mechanisms are used to reduce the data set size.

Numerosity reduction: where the data are replaced or estimated by alternative, smaller data representations such as parametric models (which need store only the model parameters instead

Discretization and concept hierarchy generation: where raw data values for attributes are replaced by ranges or higher conceptual levels. Data discretization is a form of numerosity reduction that is very useful for the automatic generation of concept hierarchies. Discretization and concept hierarchy generation are powerful tools for data mining, in that they allow the mining of data at multiple levels of abstraction.

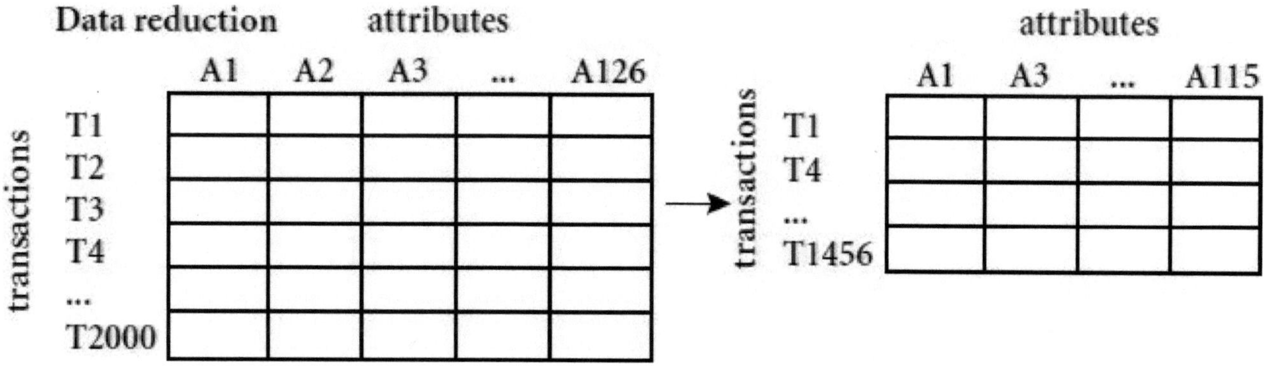

Data reduction

attributes

transactions

	A1	A2	A3	...	A126
T1					
T2					
T3					
T4					
...					
T2000					

→

attributes

transactions

	A1	A3	...	A115
T1				
T4				
...				
T1456				

V

Apriori Algorithm

Apriori Algorithm

Purpose: The Apriori Algorithm is an influential algorithm for mining frequent itemsets for boolean association rules.

Key Concepts:

Frequent Itemsets: The sets of item which has minimum support (denoted by Li for ith-Itemset).

Apriori Property: Any subset of frequent itemset must be frequent.

Join Operation: To find Lk, a set of candidate k-itemsets is generated by joining Lk-1 itself.

Find the frequent itemsets: the sets of items that have minimum support – A subset of a frequent itemset must also be a frequent itemset (Apriori Property)

i.e., if {AB} is a frequent itemset, both {A} and {B} should be a frequent itemset – Iteratively find frequent itemsets with cardinality from 1 to k (k-itemset)

Use the frequent itemsets to generate association rules.

The Apriori Algorithm : Pseudo code

Join Step: C k is generated by joining Lk-1with itself

Prune Step: Any (k-1)-itemset that is not frequent cannot be a subset of a frequent k-itemset

Pseudo-code:

Ck: Candidate itemset of size k Lk: frequent itemset of size k L1= {frequent items};

for (k = 1; Lk != ∅; k++) do begin

Ck+1 = candidates generated from Lk;

for each transaction t in database do

Increment the count of all candidates in Ck+1 That are contained in t

Lk+1 = candidates in Ck+1 with min_support

end

return ?k Lk;

TID	List of Items
T100	I1, I2, I5
T100	I2, I4
T100	I2, I3
T100	I1, I2, I4
T100	I1, I3
T100	I2, I3
T100	I1, I3
T100	I1, I2 ,I3, I5
T100	I1, I2, I3

Example

- Consider a database, D, consisting of 9 transactions.
- Suppose min. support count required is 2
  (i.e. min_sup = 2/9 = 22 %)
- Let minimum confidence required is 70%.
- We have to first find out the frequent itemset using Apriori algorithm.
- Then, Association rules will be generated using min. support & min. confidence.

➤ **Step 1: Generating 1-itemset Frequent Pattern**

Scan D for count of each candidate

Itemset	Sup Count
{I1}	6
{I2}	7
{I3}	6
{I4}	2
{I5}	2

C_1

Compare candidate support count with minimum support count

Itemset	Sup Count
{I1}	6
{I2}	7
{I3}	6
{I4}	2
{I5}	2

L_1

- The set of frequent 1-itemsets, L_1, consists of the candidate 1- itemsets satisfying minimu support.
- In the first iteration of the algorithm, each item is a member of the set of candidate.

➤ **Step 2: Generating 2-itemset Frequent Pattern**

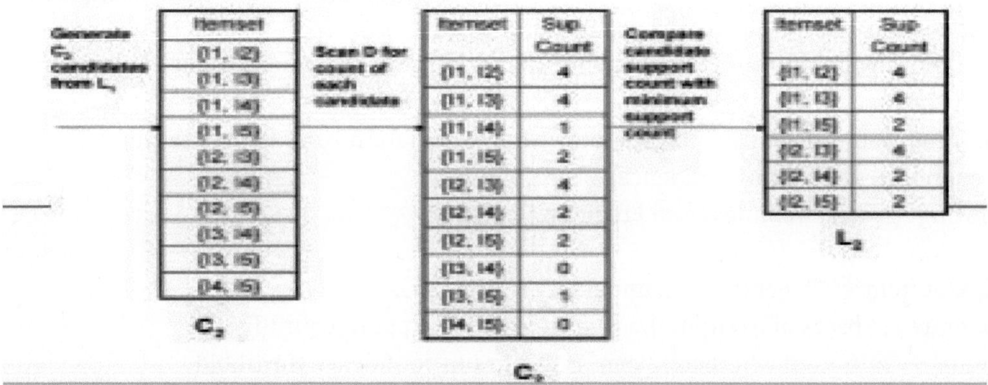

Itemset
{I1, I2}
{I1, I3}
{I1, I4}
{I1, I5}
{I2, I3}
{I2, I4}
{I2, I5}
{I3, I4}
{I3, I5}
{I4, I5}

C_2

Itemset	Sup Count
{I1, I2}	4
{I1, I3}	4
{I1, I4}	1
{I1, I5}	2
{I2, I3}	4
{I2, I4}	2
{I2, I5}	2
{I3, I4}	0
{I3, I5}	1
{I4, I5}	0

C_2

Itemset	Sup Count
{I1, I2}	4
{I1, I3}	4
{I1, I5}	2
{I2, I3}	4
{I2, I4}	2
{I2, I5}	2

L_2

To discover the set of frequent 2-itemsets, L2, the algorithm uses L1 Join L1 to generate a candidate set of 2-itemsets, C2.

Next, the transactions in D are scanned and the support count for each candidate itemset in C2 is accumulated (as shown in the middle table).

The set of frequent 2-itemsets, L2, is then determined, consisting of those candidate 2-itemsets in C2 having minimum support.

Note: We haven't used Apriori Property yet.

Step 3: Generating 3-itemset Frequent Pattern

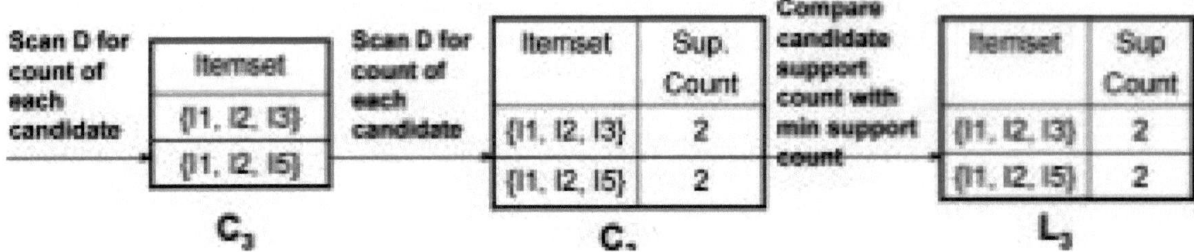

The generation of the set of candidate 3-itemsets, C3 , involves use of the Apriori Property.

In order to find C3, we compute L2 Join L2.

o C3 = L2 join L2 = {{I1, I2, I3}, {I1, I2, I5}, {I1, I3, I5}, {I2, I3, I4}, {I2, I3, I5}, {I2, I4, I5}}.

Now, Join step is complete and Prune step will be used to reduce the size of C3. Prune step helps to avoid heavy computation due to large Ck.

Based on the Apriori property that all subsets of a frequent itemset must also be frequent, we can determine that four latter candidates cannot possibly be frequent. How ?

For example, lets take {I1, I2, I3}. The 2-item subsets of it are {I1, I2}, {I1, I3} & {I2, I3}. Since all 2- item subsets of {I1, I2, I3} are members of L2, We will keep {I1, I2, I3} in C3.

Lets take another example of {I2, I3, I5} which shows how the pruning is performed. The 2-item subsets are {I2, I3}, {I2, I5} & {I3,I5}.

But, {I3, I5} is not a member of L2 and hence it is not frequent violating Apriori Property. Thus We will have to remove {I2, I3, I5} from C3.

Therefore, C3 = {{I1, I2, I3}, {I1, I2, I5}} after checking for all members of result of Join operation for Pruning.

Now, the transactions in D are scanned in order to determine L3, consisting of those candidates 3- itemsets in C3 having minimum support.

Step 4: Generating 4-itemset Frequent Pattern

The algorithm uses L3 Join L3 to generate a candidate set of 4-itemsets, C4. Although the join results in {{I1, I2, I3, I5}}, this itemset is pruned since its subset {{I2, I3, I5}} is not frequent.

Thus, C4 = φ, and algorithm terminates, having found all of the frequent items. This completes our Apriori Algorithm. What's Next?

These frequent itemsets will be used to generate strong association rules (where strong association rules satisfy both minimum support & minimum confidence).

Step 5: Generating Association Rules from Frequent Itemsets

Procedure:

For each frequent itemset "l", generate all nonempty subsets of l.

For every nonempty subset s of l, output the rule "s -> (l-s)" if support_count(l) /

support_count(s) >= min_conf where min_conf is minimum confidence threshold.

Back to Example:

o We had L = {{I1}, {I2}, {I3}, {I4}, {I5}, {I1, I2}, {I1, I3}, {I1, I5}, {I2, I3}, {I2, I4}, {I2, I5}, {I1, I2, I3}, {I1, I2, I5}}.

Let's take l = {I1, I2, I5}. – It's all nonempty subsets are {I1, I2}, {I1, I5}, {I2, I5}, {I1}, {I2}, {I5}.

Let minimum confidence threshold is, say 70%.

The resulting association rules are shown below, each listed with its confidence.

R1: I1 ^ I2 -> I5 Confidence = sc{I1, I2, I5}/sc{I1,I2} = 2/4 = 50% (R1 is Rejected)

R2: I1 ^ I5 -> I2 Confidence = sc{I1, I2, I5}/sc{I1,I5} = 2/2 = 100% (R2 is Selected)

R3: I2 ^ I5 -> I1 Confidence = sc{I1, I2, I5}/sc{I2,I5} = 2/2 = 100% (R3 is Selected)

R4: I1 -> I2 ^ I5 Confidence = sc{I1, I2, I5}/sc{I1} = 2/6 = 33% (R4 is Rejected)

R5: I2 -> I1 ^ I5 Confidence = sc{I1, I2, I5}/{I2} = 2/7 = 29% (R5 is Rejected)

R6: I5 -> I1 ^ I2 Confidence = sc{I1, I2, I5}/ {I5} = 2/2 = 100% (R6 is Selected)

In this way, we have found three strong association rules.

Methods to Improve Apriori's Efficiency

Hash-based itemset cunting:

A k-itemset whose corresponding hashing bucket count is below the threshold cannot be frequent.

Transactin reductin:

A transaction that does not contain any frequent k-itemset is useless in subsequent scans.

Partitining:

Any itemset that is potentially frequent in DB must be frequent in at least one of the partitions of DB.

Sampling:

mining on a subset of given data, lower support threshold + a method to determine the completeness.

Dynamic itemset cunting:

add new candidate itemsets only when all of their subsets are estimated to be frequent.

Market Basket Analysis

Market Basket Analysis is a modelling technique based upon the theory that if you buy a certain group of items, you are more (or less) likely to buy another group of items. For example, if you are in a store and you buy a milk and don't buy a bread, you are more likely to buy eggs at the same time than somebody who didn't buy bread.

The set of items a customer buys is referred to as an itemset, and market basket analysis seeks to find relationships between purchases.

Typically, the relationship will be in the form of a rule:

e.g IF {milk, eggs} THEN {bread}.

The probability that a customer will buy milk without an eggs (i.e. that the antecedent is true) is referred to as the support for the rule. The conditional probability that a customer will purchase bread is referred to as the confidence.

The algorithms for performing market basket analysis are fairly straightforward. The complexities mainly arise in exploiting taxonomies, avoiding combinatorial explosions (a supermarket may stock 10,000 or more line items), and dealing with the large amounts of transaction data that may be available.

A major difficulty is that a large number of the rules found may be trivial for anyone familiar with the business. Although the volume of data has been reduced, we are still asking the user to find a needle in a haystack.

Requiring rules to have a high minimum support level and a high confidence level risks missing any exploitable result we might have found. One partial solution to this problem is differential market basket analysis, as described below.

How is it used?

In retailing, most purchases are bought on impulse. Market basket analysis gives clues as to what a customer might have bought if the idea had occurred to them.

As a first step, therefore, market basket analysis can be used in deciding the location and promotion of goods inside a store. If, as has been observed, purchasers of Barbie dolls have are more likely to buy candy, then high-margin candy can be placed near to the Barbie doll display. Customers who would have bought candy with their Barbie dolls had they thought of it will now be suitably tempted.

But this is only the first level of analysis. Differential market basket analysis can find interesting results and can also eliminate the problem of a potentially high volume of trivial results.

In differential analysis, we compare results between different stores, between customers in different demographic groups, between different days of the week, different seasons of the year, etc.

If we observe that a rule holds in one store, but not in any other (or does not hold in one store, but holds in all others), then we know that there is something interesting about that store. Perhaps its clientele is different, or perhaps it has organized its displays in a novel and more lucrative way. Investigating such differences may yield useful insights which will improve company sales.

Application AreasAlthough Market Basket Analysis conjures up pictures of shopping carts and supermarket shoppers, it is important to realize that there are many other areas in which it can be applied. These include:

VI

Classification and Prediction

Classification and Prediction

There are two forms of data analysis that can be used for extracting models describing important classes or to predict future data trends.

These two forms are as follows

Classification

Prediction

Classification models predict categorical class labels.

Prediction models predict continuous valued functions.

We can build a classification model to categorize bank loan applications as either safe or risky.

Prediction model to predict the expenditures in dollars of potential customers on computer equipment given their income and occupation.

classification?

Following are the examples of cases where the data analysis task is Classification –

A bank loan officer wants to analyze the data in order to know which customer (loan applicant) are risky or which are safe.

A marketing manager at a company needs to analyze a customer with a given profile, who will buy a new computer.

In both of the above examples, a model or classifier is constructed to predict the categorical labels. These labels are risky or safe for loan application data and yes or no for marketing data.

What is prediction?

Following are the examples of cases where the data analysis task is Prediction –

Suppose the marketing manager needs to predict how much a given customer will spend during a sale at his company.

In this example we are bothered to predict a numeric value. Therefore the data analysis task is an example of numeric prediction.

In this case, a model or a predictor will be constructed that predicts a continuous-valued-function or ordered value.

Classification and Prediction Issues

The major issue is preparing the data for Classification and Prediction. Preparing the data involves the following activities –

Data Cleaning

Data cleaning involves removing the noise and treatment of missing values.

The noise is removed by applying smoothing techniques and the problem of missing values is solved by replacing a missing value with most commonly occurring value for that attribute.

Relevance Analysis

Database may also have the irrelevant attributes. Correlation analysis is used to know whether any two given attributes are related.

Data Transformation and reduction

The data can be transformed by any of the following methods.

Normalization

The data is transformed using normalization.

Normalization involves scaling all values for given attribute in order to make them fall within a small specified range.

Normalization is used when in the learning step, the neural networks or the methods involving measurements are used.

Generalization

The data can also be transformed by generalizing it to the higher concept.

For this purpose we can use the concept hierarchies.

Comparison of Classification and Prediction Methods

Here is the criteria for comparing the methods of Classification and Prediction –

Accuracy – Accuracy of classifier refers to the ability of classifier. It predict the class label correctly and the accuracy of the predictor refers to how well a given predictor can guess the value of predicted attribute for a new data.

Speed – this refers to the computational cost in generating and using the classifier or predictor.

Robustness – It refers to the ability of classifier or predictor to make correct predictions from given noisy data.

Scalability – Scalability refers to the ability to construct the classifier or predictor efficiently; given large amount of data.

Interpretability – It refers to what extent the classifier or predictor understands.

Rule based classification

Rule-based classifier makes use of a set of IF-THEN rules for classification.

We can express a rule in the following from

Let us consider a rule R1,

IF condition THEN conclusion

R1: IF age=youth AND student=yes THEN buy_computer=yes

The IF part of the rule is called rule antecedent or precondition.

The THEN part of the rule is called rule consequent.

The antecedent part the condition consist of one or more attribute tests and these tests are logically ANDed.

The consequent part consists of class prediction.

We can also write rule R1 as follows:

R1: (age = youth) ^ (student = yes))(buys_computer = yes)

If the condition (that is, all of the attribute tests) in a rule antecedent holds true for a given tuple, we say that the rule antecedent is satisfied (or simply, that the rule is satisfied) and that the rule covers the tuple.

A rule R can be assessed by its coverage and accuracy.

Given a tuple, X, from a class labeled data set D, let ncovers be the number of tuples covered by R; ncorrect be the number of tuples correctly classified by R; and |D| be the number of tuples in D.

We can define the coverage and accuracy of R as

That is, a rule's coverage is the percentage of tuples that are covered by the rule (i.e. whose attribute values hold true for the rule's antecedent).

For a rule's accuracy, we look at the tuples that it covers and see what percentage of them the rule can correctly classify.

We can use rule-based classification to predict the class label of a given tuple X.

If a rule is satisfied by X, the rule is said to be triggered.

For example, suppose we have

X= (age = youth, income = medium, student = yes, credit rating = fair)

We would like to classify X according to buys_computer. X satisfies R1, which triggers the rule.

If R1 is the only rule satisfied, then the rule fires by returning the class prediction for X.

If more than one rule is triggered, we need a conflict resolution strategy to figure out which rule gets to fire and assign its class prediction to X.

There are many possible strategies. We look at two, namely size ordering and rule ordering.

Size ordering

The size ordering scheme assigns the highest priority to the triggering rule that has the "toughest" requirements, where toughness is measured by the rule antecedent size.

That is, the triggering rule with the most attribute tests is fired.

Rule ordering

The rule ordering scheme prioritizes the rules beforehand. The ordering may be class based or rule- based.

With class-based ordering, the classes are sorted in order of decreasing "importance," such as by decreasing order of prevalence.

That is, all of the rules for the most prevalent (or most frequent) class come first, the rules for the next prevalent class come next, and so on.

With rule-based ordering, the rules are organized into one long priority list, according to some measure of rule quality such as accuracy, coverage, or size (number of attribute tests in the rule antecedent), or based on advice from domain experts.

When rule ordering is used, the rule set is known as a decision list.

With rule ordering, the triggering rule that appears earliest in the list has highest priority, and so it gets to fire its class prediction.

Any other rule that satisfies X is ignored. Most rule-based classification systems use a class-based rule-ordering strategy.

What are neural networks? List strengths and weakness of neural network as classifier.

Neural Network is a set of connected INPUT/OUTPUT UNITS, where each connection has a WEIGHT associated with it.

Neural Network learning is also called CONNECTIONIST learning due to the connections between units.

It is a case of SUPERVISED, INDUCTIVE or CLASSIFICATION learning.

Neural Network learns by adjusting the weights so as to be able to correctly classify the training data and hence, after testing phase, to classify unknown data.

Strengths of Neural Network:

It can handle against complex data. (i.e., problems with many parameters)

It can handle noise in the training data.

The Prediction accuracy is generally high.

Neural Networks are robust, work well even when training examples contain errors.

Neural Networks can handle missing data well.

The greatest power of Neural Networks is that it is endowed with a finite number of hidden units, can yet approximate any continuous function to any desired degree of accuracy. This has been commonly referred to as the property of universal approximation.

No prior knowledge of the data generating process is needed for implementing Neural Network.

Problem of model misspecification does not occur.

In case of Neural Network since no specifications are used as the network merely learns the hidden relationship in the data.

Weakness of Neural Network:

Neural Network implementations are slow in the training phase.

A major disadvantage of neural network lies in their knowledge representation.

Acquired knowledge in the form of a network units connected by weighted links is difficult for humans to interpret.

This factor has motivated research in extracting the knowledge embedded in trained neural network and in representing it in forms of symbolic rules.

The addition of too many hidden units incites the problem of over fitting the data; meaning that the network learns too well in the training data session but generates inferior results in case of out of sample session.

The construction of the NN model can be a time consuming process since building up the Neural Network architecture is synonymous to a strenuous activity involving trial and error.

What is Regression

Regression is a data mining function that predicts a number.

Age, weight, distance, temperature, income, or sales could all be predicted using regression techniques.

For example, a regression model could be used to predict children's height, given their age, weight, and other factors.

A regression task begins with a data set in which the target values are known.

For example, a regression model that predicts children's height could be developed based on observed data for many children over a period of time.

The data might track age, height, weight, developmental milestones, family history, and so on.

Height would be the target, the other attributes would be the predictors, and the data for each child would constitute a case.

Regression models are tested by computing various statistics that measure the difference between the predicted values and the expected values.

It is required to understand the mathematics used in regression analysis to develop quality regression models for data mining.

The goal of regression analysis is to determine the values of parameters for a function that cause the function to best fit a set of data observations that you provide.

It shows that regression is the process of estimating the value of a continuous target (y) as a function (F)

of one or more predictors (x1 , x2 , ..., xn), a set of parameters (θ1 , θ2 , ..., θn), and a measure of error (e).

$y = F(x,\theta) + e$

The process of training a regression model involves finding the best parameter values for the function that minimize a measure of the error.

Linear Regression

The simplest form of regression to visualize is linear regression with a single predictor.

A linear regression technique can be used if the relationship between x and y can be approximated with a straight line.

Linear regression with a single predictor can be expressed with the following equation.

$y = \theta 2x + \theta 1 + e$

The regression parameters in simple linear regression are:

The slope of the line (θ) — the angle between a data point and the regression line

The y intercept (θ) — the point where x crosses the y axis (x = 0)

Figure 4-1 Linear Relationship Between x and y

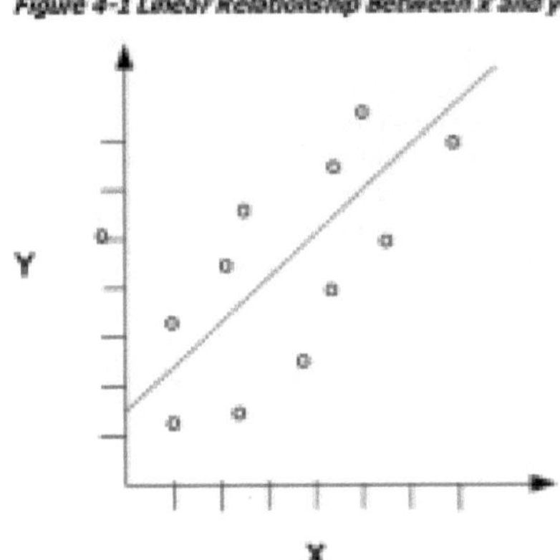

Nonlinear Regression

- Often the relationship between x and y cannot be approximated with a straight line.
- In this case, a nonlinear regression technique may be used. Alternatively, the data could be preprocessed to make the relationship linear.

Figure 4-2 Nonlinear Relationship Between x and y

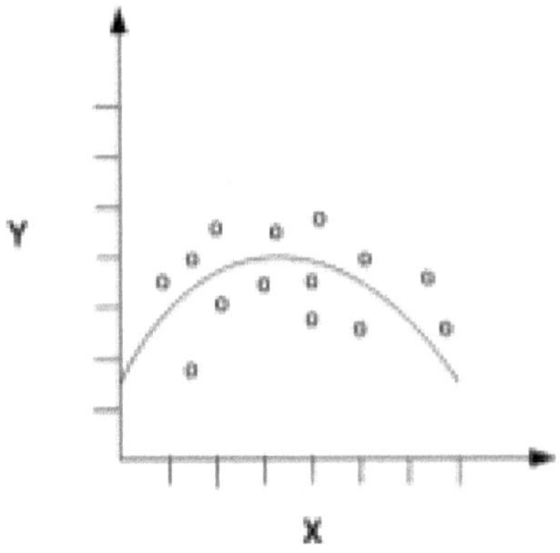

Briefly outline the major steps of decision tree classification.

A decision tree is a structure that includes a root node, branches, and leaf nodes.

Each internal node denotes a test on an attribute, each branch denotes the outcome of a test, and each leaf node holds a class label. The topmost node in the tree is the root node.

The following decision tree is for the concept buy_computer that indicates whether a customer at a company is likely to buy a computer or not.

Each internal node represents a test on an attribute.

Each leaf node represents a class.

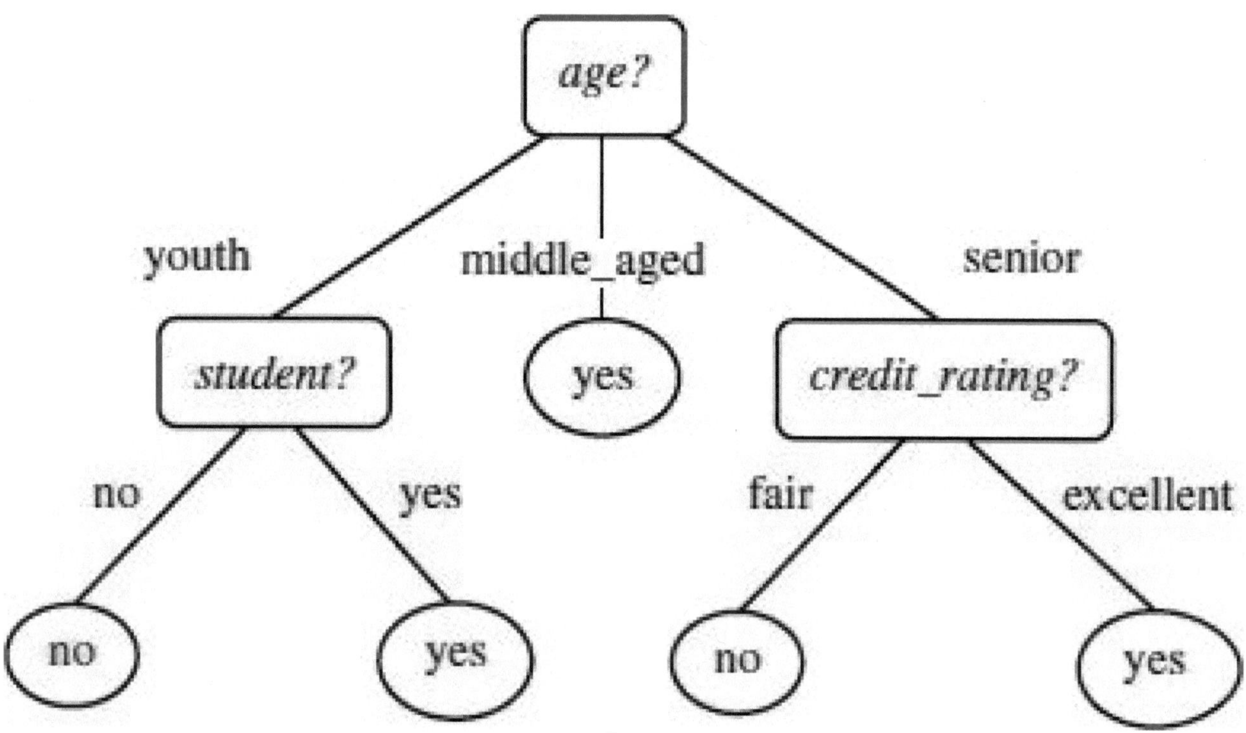

The benefits of having a decision tree are as follows –

It does not require any domain knowledge.

It is easy to comprehend.

The learning and classification steps of a decision tree are simple and fast.

A basic algorithm for learning decision trees is as below.

During tree construction, attribute selection measures are used to select the attribute that best partitions the tuples into distinct classes.

When decision trees are built, many of the branches may reflect noise or outliers in the training data.

Tree pruning attempts to identify and remove such branches, with the goal of improving classification accuracy on unseen data.

Algorithm: Generate decision tree. Generate a decision tree from the training tuples of data partition D.

Input:

Data partition, D, which is a set of training tuples and their associated class labels;

attribute list, the set of candidate attributes;

Attribute selection method, a procedure to determine the splitting criterion that "best" partitions the data tuples into individual classes. This criterion consists of a splitting attribute and, possibly, either a split point or splitting subset.

Output: A decision tree.

Method:

create a node N;

if tuples in D are all of the same class, C then

return N as a leaf node labeled with the class C;

if attribute list is empty then

return N as a leaf node labeled with the majority class in D; // majority voting

apply Attribute selection method(D, attribute list) to find the "best" splitting criterion;

label node N with splitting criterion;

if splitting attribute is discrete-valued and multi way splits allowed then // not restricted to binary trees
attribute list attribute list splitting attribute; // remove splitting attribute
for each outcome j of splitting criterion // partition the tuples and grow sub trees for each partition
let Dj be the set of data tuples in D satisfying outcome j; // a partition
if Dj is empty then
attach a leaf labeled with the majority class in D to node N;
else attach the node returned by Generate decision tree(Dj, attribute list) to node N; endfor
return N;
Logistic Regression.

- The prediction is based on the use of one or several predictors (numerical and categorical).
- Logistic regression predicts the probability of an outcome that can only have two values (i.e. a dichotomy) A linear regression is not appropriate for predicting the value of a binary variable for two reasons:
- Logistic regression is similar to a linear regression, but the curve is constructed using the natural logarithm
- A logistic regression produces a logistic curve, which is limited to values between 0 and 1.
- A linear regression will predict values outside the acceptable range (e.g. predicting probabilities outside the range 0 to 1).
- Since the dichotomous experiments can only have one of two possible values for each experiment, the residuals will not be normally distributed about the predicted line. of the "odds" of the target variable, rather than the probability.
- Moreover, the predictors do not have to be normally distributed or have equal variance in each group.
- In the logistic regression the constant (b0) moves the curve left and right and the slope (b1) defines the steepness of the curve.
- Advantage of logistic regression is that the algorithm is highly flexible, taking any kind of input, and supports several different analytical tasks:

    - Use demographics to make predictions about outcomes, such as risk for a certain disease.
    - Explore and weight the factors that contribute to a result. For example, find the factors that influence customers to make a repeat visit to a store.
    - Classify documents, e-mail, or other objects that have many attributes.

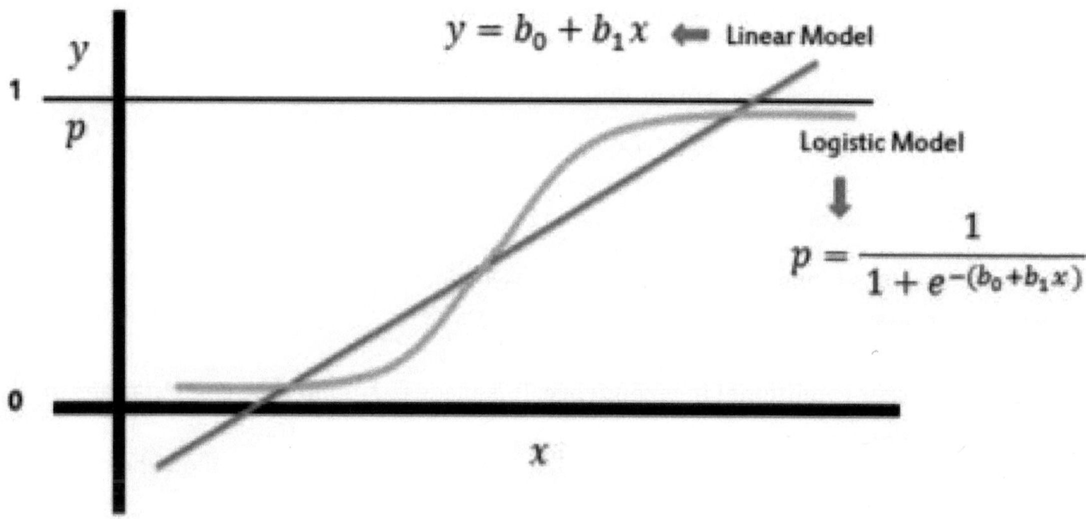

DB Miner /WEKA/DTREG Tools. DB Miner

- By incorporation of several interesting data mining techniques, including attribute-oriented induction, progressive deepening for mining multiple-level rules, and meta-rule guided knowledge mining, the system provides a user-friendly, interactive data mining environment with good performance.
- The system implements a wide spectrum of data mining functions, including generalization, characterization, discrimination, association, classification, and prediction.
- DBMiner, a data mining system for interactive mining of multiple-level knowledge in large relational databases, has been developed based on our years-of-research.

WEKA

- Weka is a collection of machine learning algorithms for data mining tasks.
- The algorithms can either be applied directly to a dataset or called from your own Java code.
- Weka contains tools for data pre-processing, classification, regression, clustering, association rules, and visualization.
- It is also well-suited for developing new machine learning schemes.

DTREG

- It is a robust application that is installed easily on any Windows system.
- DTREG reads Comma Separated Value (CSV) data files that are easily created from almost any data source. Once you create your data file, just feed it into DTREG, and let DTREG do all of the work of creating a decision tree, Support Vector Machine, K-Means clustering, Linear Discriminant Function, Linear Regression or Logistic Regression model. Even complex analyses can be set up in minutes.
- Classification and Regression Trees. DTREG can build Classification Trees where the target variable being predicted is categorical and Regression Trees where the target variable is continuous like income or sales volume.

Naïve Bayesian classification.

- Bayesian classifiers can predict class membership probabilities, such as the probability that a given tuple belongs to a particular class.
- Bayesian classification is based on Bayes' theorem, described below.
-

Why it is called naïve?

- Bayesian classifiers have also exhibited high accuracy and speed when applied to large databases.
- Naïve Bayesian classifiers assume that the effect of an attribute value on a given class is independent of the values of the other attributes.
- This assumption is called *class* **conditional independence.** It is made to simplify the computations involved and, in this sense, is considered **"naïve".**
- *Bayesian belief networks* are graphical models, which unlike naïve Bayesian classifiers allow the representation of dependencies among subsets of attributes.
- Bayesian belief networks can also be used for classification.
- In Bayesian terms, $\boldsymbol{X}$ is considered "evidence".
- As usual, it is described by measurements made on a set of n attributes.
- Let H be some hypothesis, such as that the data tuple $\mathbf{X}$ belongs to a specified class C.
- For classification problems, we want to determine $P(H|\mathbf{X})$, the probability that the hypothesis H holds given the "evidence" or observed data tuple $\mathbf{X}$.

- In other words, we are looking for the probability that tuple $\mathbf{X}$ belongs to class C, given that we know the attribute description of $\mathbf{X}$.

Supervised learning, training set, testing set, accuracy of classifier, sensitivity, and regression. Supervised learning:

- In supervised learning, each example is a pair consisting of an input object (typically a vector) and a desired output value (also called the supervisory signal).
- The training data consist of a set of training examples.
- Supervised learning is the machine learning task of inferring a function from labeled training data.

Training set:

- A training set is a set of data used in various areas of information science to discover potentially predictive relationships.
- Training sets are used in artificial intelligence, machine learning, genetic programming, intelligentsystems, and statistics.
- In all these fields, a training set has much the same role and is often used in conjunction with a test set.

Testing set:

- A **test set** is a set of data used in various areas of information science to assess the strength and utility of a predictive relationship.

- Test sets are used in artificial intelligence, machine learning, genetic programming and statistics. In all these fields, a test set has much the same role.

Accuracy of classifier:

- In the fields of science, engineering, industry, and statistics, the accuracy of a measurement system is the degree of closeness of measurements of a quantity to that quantity's actual (true) value.

Sensitivity analysis:

- Local Sensitivity as correlation coefficients and partial derivatives can only use, if the correlation between input and output is linear.

Regression:

- In statistics, **regression analysis** is a statistical process for estimating the relationships among variables.
- It includes many techniques for modeling and analyzing several variables, when the focus is on the relationship between a dependent variable and one or more independent variables.
- More specifically, regression analysis helps one understand how the typical value of the dependent variable (or 'criterion variable') changes when any one of the independent variables is varied, while the other independent variables are held fixed.

VII

Data Mining for Business Intelligence Applications

Data Analytics Life Cycle

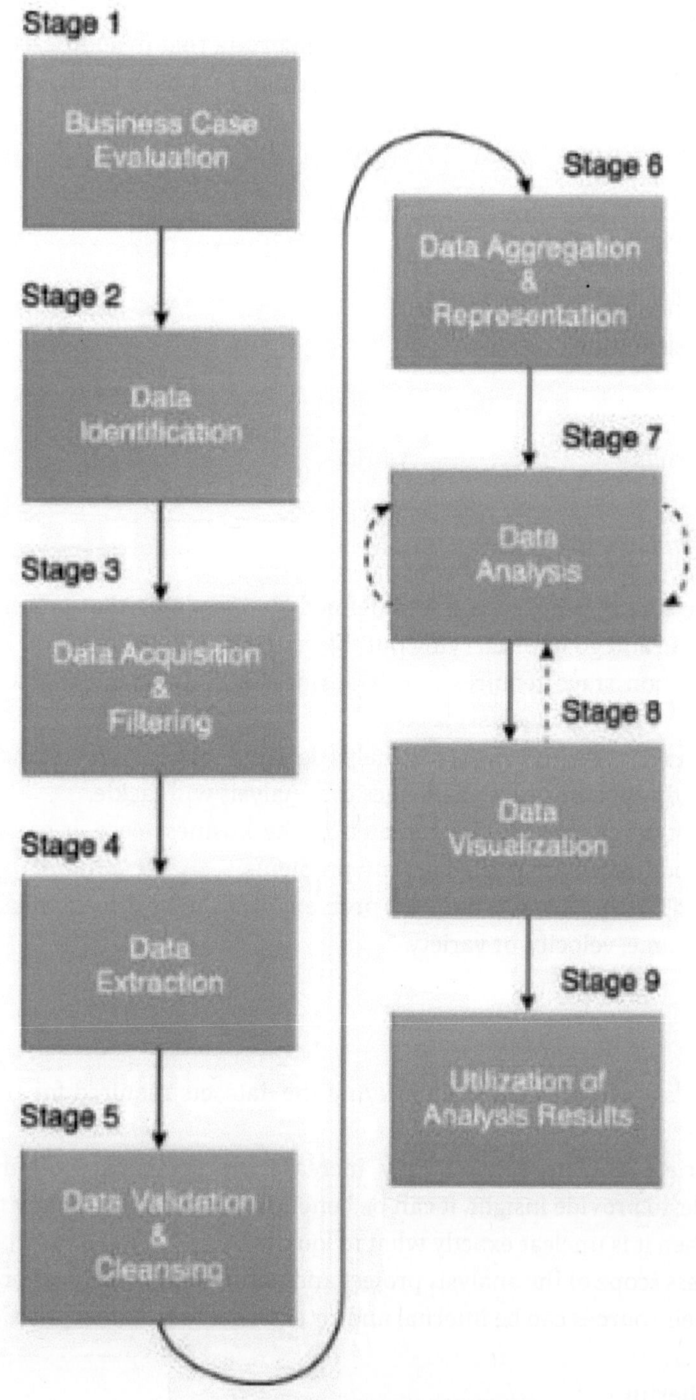

Data Analytics life cycle

- Big Data analysis differs from traditional data analysis primarily due to the volume, velocity and variety characteristics of the data being processes.
- To address the distinct requirements for performing analysis on Big Data, a step-by-step methodology is needed to organize the activities and tasks involved with acquiring, processing, analyzing and repurposing data.

- The upcoming sections explore a specific data analytics lifecycle that organizes and manages the tasks and activities associated with the analysis of Big Data.
- From a Big Data adoption and planning perspective, it is important that in addition to the lifecycle, consideration be made for issues of training, education, tooling and staffing of a data analytics team. he Big Data analytics lifecycle can be divided into the following nine stages,
- Business Case Evaluation
- Data Identification
- Data Acquisition & Filtering
- Data Extraction
- Data Validation & Cleansing
- Data Aggregation & Representation
- Data Analysis
- Data Visualization
- Utilization of Analysis Results

Business Case Evaluation

- Big Data analytics lifecycle must begin with a well-defined business case that presents a clear understanding of the justification, motivation and goals of carrying out the analysis.
- The Business Case Evaluation stage requires that a business case be created, assessed and approved prior to proceeding with the actual hands-on analysis tasks.
- An evaluation of a Big Data analytics business case helps decision-makers understand the business resources that will need to be utilized and which business challenges the analysis will tackle.
- Based on business requirements that are documented in the business case, it can be determined whether the business problems being addressed are really Big Data problems.
- In order to qualify as a Big Data problem, a business problem needs to be directly related to one or more of the Big Data characteristics of volume, velocity, or variety.

Data Identification

- The Data Identification stage is dedicated to identifying the datasets required for the analysis project and their sources.
- Identifying a wider variety of data sources may increase the probability of finding hidden patterns and correlations. For example, to provide insight, it can be beneficial to identify as many types of related data sources as possible, especially when it is unclear exactly what to look for.
- Depending on the business scope of the analysis project and nature of the business problems being addressed, the required datasets and their sources can be internal and/or external to the enterprise.

Data Acquisition and Filtering

- During the Data Acquisition and Filtering stage, the data is gathered from all of the data sources that were identified during the previous stage.
- The acquired data is then subjected to automated filtering for the removal of corrupt data or data that has been deemed to have no value to the analysis objectives.
- Depending on the type of data source, data may come as a collection of files, such as data purchased from a third-party data provider, or may require API integration, such as with Twitter.
- In many cases, especially where external, unstructured data is concerned, some or most of the acquired data may be irrelevant (noise) and can be discarded as part of the filtering process.

Data Extraction

- The Data Extraction lifecycle stage is dedicated to extracting disparate data and transforming it into a format that the underlying Big Data solution can use for the purpose of the data analysis.
  - The extent of extraction and transformation required depends on the types of analytics and capabilities of the Big Data solution.
  - For example, extracting the required fields from delimited textual data, such as with webserver log files, may not be necessary if the underlying Big Data solution can already directly process those files.

- Data Validation and Cleansing
- The Data Validation and Cleansing stage is dedicated to establishing often complex validation rules and removing any known invalid data.
- Big Data solutions often receive redundant data across different datasets.
- This redundancy can be exploited to explore interconnected datasets in order to assemble validation parameters and fill in missing valid data.

Data Aggregation and Representation

- The Data Aggregation and Representation stage is dedicated to integrating multiple datasets together to arrive at a unified view.
- Performing this stage can become complicated because of differences in:
- Data Structure – Although the data format may be the same, the data model may be different.
- Semantics – A value that is labeled differently in two different datasets may mean the same
- thing, for example "surname" and "last name."
- The large volumes processed by Big Data solutions can make data aggregation a time and effort- intensive operation.
- Reconciling these differences can require complex logic that is executed automatically without the need for human intervention.

Data Analysis

- The Data Analysis stage is dedicated to carrying out the actual analysis task, which typically involves one or more types of analytics.
- This stage can be iterative in nature, especially if the data analysis is exploratory, in which case analysis is repeated until the appropriate pattern or correlation is uncovered.
- The exploratory analysis approach will be explained shortly, along with confirmatory analysis.

Data Visualization

- The Data Visualization stage is dedicated to using data visualization techniques and tools to graphically communicate the analysis results for effective interpretation by business users.
- The results of completing the Data Visualization stage provide users with the ability to perform visual analysis, allowing for the discovery of answers to questions that users have not yet even formulated.

Utilization of Analysis Results

- The Utilization of Analysis Results stage is dedicated to determining how and where processed analysis data can be further leveraged.
- Depending on the nature of the analysis problems being addressed, it is possible for the analysis results to produce "models" that encapsulate new insights and understandings about the nature of the patterns and relationships that exist within the data that was analyzed.

Real life applications of Data Mining and Business Intelligence.

- As the importance of data analytics continues to grow, companies are depending more and more applications for Data Mining and Business Intelligence.
- Here we take a look at real life applications of these technologies and shed light on the benefits they can bring to your business.

Service providers

- The first example of Data Mining and Business Intelligence comes from service providers in the mobile phone and utilities industries.
- Mobile phone and utilities companies use Data Mining and Business Intelligence to predict 'churn', the terms they use for when a customer leaves their company to get their phone/gas/broadband from another provider.
- They collate billing information, customer services interactions, website visits and other metrics to give each customer a probability score, then target offers and incentives to customers whom they perceive to be at a higher risk of churning.

Retail

- Another example of Data Mining and Business Intelligence comes from the retail sector.
- Retailers segment customers into Regency, Frequency, Monetary' (RFM) groups and target marketing and promotions to those different groups.
- A customer who spends little but often and last did so recently will be handled differently to a customer who spent big but only once, and also some time ago.
- The former may receive a loyalty, upsell and cross-sell offers, whereas the latter may be offered a win- back deal, for instance.

E-commerce

- Perhaps some of the most well -known examples of Data Mining and Analytics come from E-commerce sites.
- Many Ecommerce companies use Data Mining and Business Intelligence to offer cross-sells and up-sells through their websites.
- One of the most famous of these is, Amazon, who use sophisticated mining techniques to drive there, 'People who viewed that product, also liked this' functionality.

Supermarkets

- Supermarkets provide another good example of Data Mining and Business Intelligence in action.
- Famously, supermarket loyalty card programmers are usually driven mostly, if not solely, by the desire to gather comprehensive data about customers for use in data mining.
- One notable recent example of this was with the US retailer Target.

- As part of its Data Mining program, the company developed rules to predict if their shoppers were like the specific goods.
- By looking at the contents of their customer's shopping baskets, they could spot customers who they thought were likely to be expecting and begin targeting promotions for that goods.

Crime agencies

- The use of Data Mining and Business Intelligence is not solely reserved for corporate applications and this is shown in our final example.
- Beyond corporate applications, crime prevention agencies use analytics and Data Mining to spot trends across myriads of data – helping with everything from where to deploy police manpower (where is crime most likely to happen and when?), who to search at a border crossing (based on age/type of vehicle, number/age of occupants, border crossing history) and even which intelligence to take seriously in counter-terrorism activities.

Clustering, Spatial mining, Web mining, Text mining in brief.

Cluster is a group of objects that belongs to the same class. In other words, similar objects are grouped in one cluster and dissimilar objects are grouped in another cluster."

- A cluster of data objects can be treated as one group.
- Clustering is a process of partitioning a set of data (or objects) into a set of meaningful sub-classes, called clusters.
- While doing cluster analysis, we first partition the set of data into groups based on data similarity and then assign the labels to the groups.
- The main advantage of clustering over classification is that, it is adaptable to changes and helps single out useful features that distinguish different groups.

Requirements of Clustering in Data Mining

- **Scalability** - We need highly scalable clustering algorithms to deal with large databases.
- **Ability to deal with different kinds of attributes** – Algorithms should be capable to be applied on any kind of data such as interval-based (numerical) data, categorical, and binary data.
- **Discovery of clusters with attribute shape** – the clustering algorithm should be capable of detecting clusters of arbitrary shape. They should not be bounded to only distance measures that tend to find spherical cluster of small sizes.
- **High dimensionality** – the clustering algorithm should not only be able to handle low- dimensional data but also the high dimensional space.
- **Ability to deal with noisy data** – Databases contain noisy, missing or erroneous data. Some algorithms are sensitive to such data and may lead to poor quality clusters.
- **Interpretability** – the clustering results should be interpretable, comprehensible, and usable.

Applications of Clustering

- Economic Science (especially market research).
- WWW:
- Document classification,
- Cluster Weblog data to discover groups of similar access patterns
- Pattern Recognition.
- Spatial Data Analysis: Create thematic maps in GIS by clustering feature spaces
- Image Processing

Spatial Data mining

Spatial data mining is the application of data mining to spatial models. In spatial data mining, analysts use geographical or spatial information to produce business intelligence or other results. This requires specific techniques and resources to get the geographical data into relevant and useful formats.

- Search for **spatial patterns**.
- Non-trivial search – as "automated" as possible.
- Large search space of plausible hypothesis
- Ex. Asiatic cholera: causes water, food, air and insects.
- Interesting, useful, and unexpected spatial patterns.
- Useful in certain application domain
- Ex. Shutting off identified water pump => saved human lives.
- May provide a new understanding of the world
- Ex. Water pump – Cholera connection lead to the "germ" theory.
- Spatial Data Mining Tasks
- Geo-Spatial Warehousing and OLAP
- Spatial data classification/predictive modeling
- Spatial clustering/segmentation
- Spatial association and correlation analysis
- Spatial regression analysis
- Time-related spatial pattern analysis: trends, sequential patterns, partial periodicity analysis

Web Mining

- Web mining is the use of data mining techniques to automatically discover and extract information from Web documents and services. There are three general classes of information that can be discovered by web mining: Web activity, from server logs and Web browser activity tracking.
- Web mining can be broadly divided into three distinct categories, according to the kinds of data to be mined.
- Web Content Mining
- Web Structure Mining
- Web Usage Mining
- There are three general classes of information that can be discovered by web mining:
- Web activity, from server logs and Web browser activity tracking.
- Web graph, from links between pages, people and other data.
- Web content, for the data found on Web pages and inside of documents.

Uses of Web Content Mining

- To gather, categorize, organize and provide the best possible information available on the WWW to the user requesting the information.
- To determine the relevance of the content to the search query. Improve the navigation of information on the web provides productive marketing. Produce a higher quality of information to the user.
- Understand customer behavior, evaluate effectiveness of a particular web site, and help quantify the success of a marketing campaign. Business intelligence. Competitive intelligence. Pricing analysis. Product data. Reputation.

Web mining tools

- Screen-scaper

- Automation Anywhere 6.1 (AA)
- Web Info Extractor (WIE)
- Mozenda
- Web Content Extractor (WCE)

Text Mining

- Text mining, also referred to as text data mining, roughly equivalent to text analytics, refers to the process of deriving high-quality information from text. High-quality information is typically derived through the devising of patterns and trends through means such as statistical pattern learning.

Text analysis processes

- Information retrieval or identification of a corpus is a preparatory step: collecting or identifying a set of textual materials, on the Web or held in a file system, database, or content corpus manager, for analysis.
- Although some text analytics systems apply exclusively advanced statistical methods, many others apply more extensive natural language processing, such as part of speech tagging, syntactic parsing, and other types of linguistic analysis.
- Named entity recognition is the use of gazetteers or statistical techniques to identify named text features: people, organizations, place names, stock ticker symbols, certain abbreviations, and so on. Disambiguation—the use of contextual clues—may be required to decide where, for instance, "Ford" can refer to a former U.S. president, a vehicle manufacturer, a movie star, a river crossing, or some other entity.
- Recognition of Pattern Identified Entities: Features such as telephone numbers, e-mail addresses and quantities (with units) can be discerned via regular expression or other pattern matches.
- Co - Reference: identification of noun phrases and other terms that refer to the same object.

Applications

- Enterprise Business Intelligence/Data Mining, Competitive Intelligence
- E-Discovery, Records Management
- National Security/Intelligence
- Sentiment Analysis Tools, Listening Platforms
- Natural Language/Semantic Toolkit or Service
- Publishing
- Automated ad placement
- Search/Information Access
- Social media monitoring

Explain Big Data & Characteristics of Big Data V3s in brief.

- Big Data may well be the Next Big Thing in the IT world.
- Big data burst upon the scene in the first decade of the 21st century.
- The first organizations to embrace it were online and startup firms. Firms like Google, eBay, LinkedIn, and Facebook were built around big data from the beginning.
- Like many new information technologies, big data can bring about dramatic cost reductions, substantial improvements in the time required to perform a computing task, or new product and service offerings.
- 'Big Data' is similar to 'small data', but bigger in size
- But having data bigger it requires different approaches:

Techniques, tools and architecture

- An aim to solve new problems or old problems in a better way
- Big Data generates value from the storage and processing of very large quantities of digital information that cannot be analyzed with traditional computing techniques.

Example

- Walmart handles more than 1 million customer transactions every hour.
- Facebook handles 40 billion photos from its user base.
- Decoding the human genome originally took 10 years to process; now it can be achieved in one week.
- Twitter generates 7TB of data daily.
- IBM claims 90% of today's stored data was generated in just the last two years.

How Is Big Data Different?

- Automatically generated by a machine (e.g. Sensor embedded in an engine)
- Typically, an entirely new source of data (e.g. Use of the internet)
- Not designed to be friendly (e.g. Text streams)
- May not have much values need to focus on the important part

Volume

- A typical PC might have had 10 gigabytes of storage in 2000.
- Today, Facebook ingests 500 terabytes of new data every day.
- Boeing 737 will generate 240 terabytes of flight data during a single flight across the US.
- The smart phones, the data they create and consume; sensors embedded into everyday objects will soon result in billions of new, constantly-updated data feeds containing environmental, location, and other information, including video.

Velocity

- Clickstreams and ad impressions capture user behavior at millions of events per second
- High-frequency stock trading algorithms reflect market changes within microseconds
- Machine to machine processes exchange data between billions of devices
- Infrastructure and sensors generate massive log data in real-time
- On-line gaming systems support millions of concurrent users, each producing multiple inputs per second.

Variety

- Big Data isn't just numbers, dates, and strings. Big Data is also geospatial data, 3D data, audio and video, and unstructured text, including log files and social media.
- Traditional database systems were designed to address smaller volumes of structured data, fewer updates or a predictable, consistent data structure.
- Big Data analysis includes different types of data

Benefits of Big Data

- Real-time big data isn't just a process for storing petabytes or Exabyte of data in a data warehouse, it's about the ability to make better decisions and take meaningful actions at the right time.
- Fast forward to the present and technologies like Hadoop give you the scale and flexibility to store data before you know how you are going to process it.
- Technologies such as MapReduce, Hive and Impala enable you to run queries without changing the data structures underneath.
- Now newest research finds that organizations are using big data to target customer-centric outcomes, tap into internal data and build a better information ecosystem.
- Big Data is already an important part of the $64 billion database and data analytics market.
- It offers commercial opportunities of a comparable scale to enterprise software in the late 1980s and the Internet boom of the 1990s, and the social media explosion of today.

Application of Big Data analytics

- Smarter Healthcare
- Multi-channel sales
- Homeland Security
- Traffic Control
- Manufacturing
- Telecom
- Trading Analytics

Leading Technology Vendors (Big Data)

- IBM – Netezza
- EMC – Greenplum
- Oracle – Exadata

Hadoop Architecture & Storage

- Hadoop, developed in 2005 and now an open source platform managed under the **Apache Software Foundation**, uses a concept known as MapReduce that is composed of two separate functions.
- The Map step inputs data and breaks it down for processing across nodes within a Hadoop instance. These "worker" nodes may in turn break the data down further for processing. In the Reduce step, the processed data is then collected back together and assembled into a format based on the original query being performed.
- To cope with truly massive-scale data analysis, Hadoop's developers implemented a scale-out architecture, based on many low-cost physical servers with distributed processing of data queries during the Map operation.
- Their logic was to **enable a Hadoop system** capable of processing many parts of a query in parallel to reduce execution times as much as possible.
- This can be contrasted with legacy-structured database design that looks to scale up within a single server by using faster processors, more memory and fast shared storage.
- Looking at the storage layer, the design aim for Hadoop is to execute the distributed processing with the minimum latency possible. This is achieved by executing Map processing on the node that stores the data, a concept known as data locality.
- As a result, Hadoop implementations can use **SATA** drives directly connected to the server, thereby keeping the overall cost of the system as low as possible.
- To implement the data storage layer, Hadoop uses a feature known as HDFS or the **Hadoop Distributed File System**. HDFS is not a file system in the traditional sense and isn't usually directly mounted for a user to view

(although there are some tools available to achieve this), which can sometimes make the concept difficult to understand; it's perhaps better to think of it simply as a Hadoop data store.

- The Hadoop Distributed File System (HDFS) is a distributed file system designed to run on commodity hardware. It has many similarities with existing distributed file systems. However, the differences from other distributed file systems are significant.
- HDFS is highly fault-tolerant and is designed to be deployed on low-cost hardware. HDFS provides high throughput access to application data and is suitable for applications that have large data sets. HDFS relaxes a few POSIX requirements to enable streaming access to file system data.

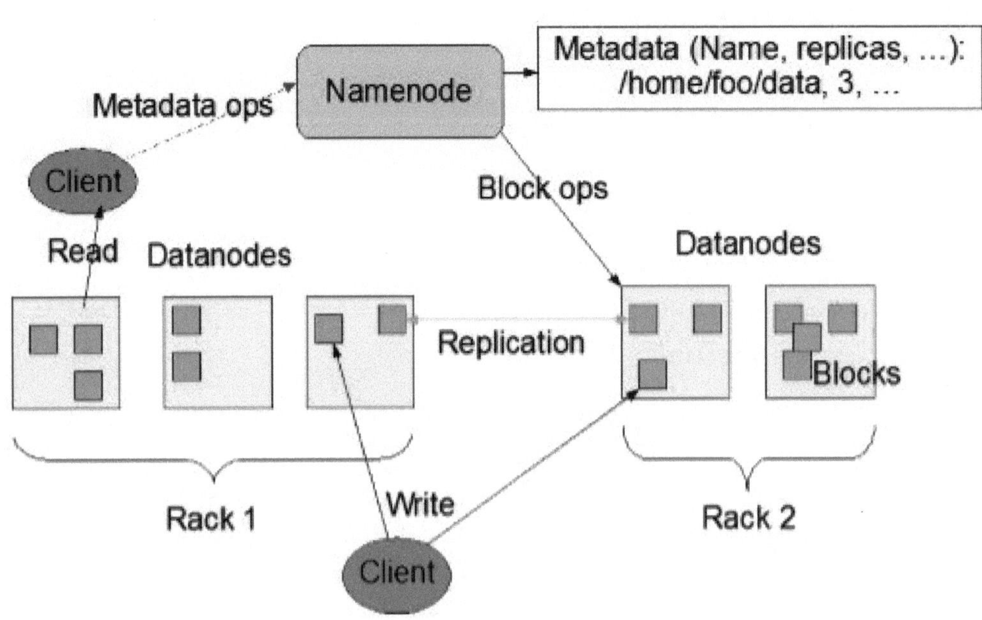

Name Node and Data Nodes

- HDFS has a master/slave architecture. An HDFS cluster consists of a single NameNode, a master server that manages the file system namespace and regulates access to files by clients.
- In addition, there are a number of DataNodes, usually one per node in the cluster, which manage storage attached to the nodes that they run on. HDFS exposes a file system namespace and allows user data to be stored in files.
- Internally, a file is split into one or more blocks and these blocks are stored in a set of DataNodes. The NameNode executes file system namespace operations like opening, closing, and renaming files and directories. It also determines the mapping of blocks to DataNodes.
- The DataNodes are responsible for serving read and write requests from the file system's clients. The
- DataNodes also perform block creation, deletion, and replication upon instruction from the NameNode.
- The existence of a single NameNode in a cluster greatly simplifies the architecture of the system. The NameNode is the arbitrator and repository for all HDFS metadata. The system is designed in such a way that user data never flows through the NameNode.

Author -1

Dr. Gaurav Kumar Ameta is a passionate academician & researcher. He is presently working as an Associate Professor in the Department of Computer Science & Engineering at Parul Institute of Technology, Parul University, Vadodara, Gujarat (India). He has more than 14 years of teaching and research experience in India and abroad in various capacities. His area of specializations is Data Mining, Machine Learning, Data Science & Cyber Security. He did his B.Tech from Rajasthan University, Jaipur and M.Tech in Computer Science & Engineering. He has done his Doctor of Philosophy (Ph.D.) in Computer Science & Engineering with specialization in Privacy Preserving Data Mining from Sir Padampat Singhania University, Udaipur (Rajasthan). He has published more than 14 research papers in National & International reputed indexed journals. Several Patents are filed by him in the fields of Machine Learning, Deep Learning, Cyber Security, Internet of Things & Communication. He has supervised more than 25 M.Tech & Ph.D. research scholars for their Project and Research work. During his academic journey he has been actively associated with IIT Mumbai & IIT Roorkee for coordinating & executing e- learning programs under National Mission on Education through ICT (NMEICT) and Virtual Labs. He has been invited as a reviewer for reviewing research papers in several International Conferences & Journals. Dr. Ameta has been invited as an academic expert for various academic & research related activities in several colleges and universities in different regions of India. He also honoured as a Judge in Smart India Hackathon. He is a lifetime member of Indian Society for Technical Education (ISTE) and Computer Society of India (CSI). He is also senior member of the international bodies like International Society for Applied Computing (ISAC), Scientific Innovation Research Group (SIRG), and International Association of Engineers (IAENG). He has also received award of academic excellence from Scientific International Publishing House.

Author -2

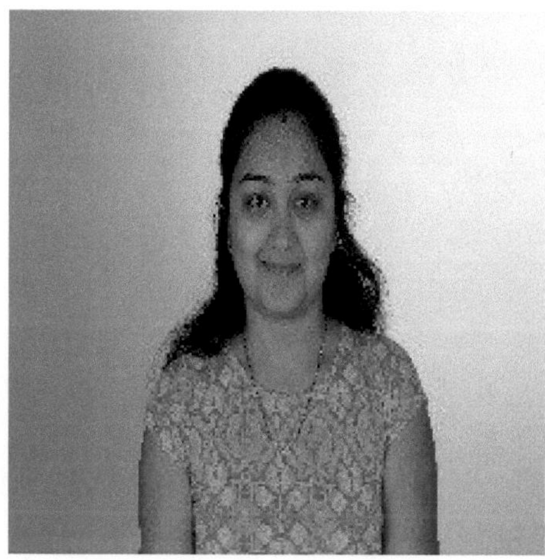

Mrs. Bhasha Anjaria, working as Assistant Professor in Department of Computer Science and Engineering at Parul Institute of Engineering, Parul University , Vadodara, Gujarat. She completed B.E (CSE) from Darshan Institute of Engineering and technology, Gujarat and M.Tech. (CSE) from Parul Institute of Engineering And Technology, Vadodara, Gujarat and Pursuing PhD in Computer Science And Engineering from Parul University, Vadodara, Gujarat. She has several publications in the field of Data Mining and Machine learning in various national and international conference as well as journals.

AUTHOR - 3

Mrs. Khushboo Trivedi, working as Assistant Professor in Department of Computer Science and Engineering at Parul Institute of Engineering, Parul University , Vadodara, Gujarat. She completed B.E (CSE) from Government Engineering College, Modasa, Gujarat And M.E (CSE) from Parul Institute of Engineering And Technology, Vadodara, Gujarat and Pursuing PhD in Computer Science And Engineering from Parul University, Vadodara, Gujarat. She has several publications in the field of Data Mining, Cloud Computing and Big Data.

Author -3

Profile

Mr. Rahul Sharma , working as Assistant Professor in Department of Computer Science and Engineering at Parul Institute of Technology, Parul University Vadodara , Gujarat. Prior to that he has more than 5+ years of teaching experience in several engineering colleges as Chameli Devi Group of Institution,Indore and Dr. A.P.J. Abdul Kalam University, he completed B.Tech (CSE) from Patel College of Science and Technology, Indore (M.P.) and M.Tech (NM&IS) from SCSIT, DAVV, Indore (M.P.). and Pursuing PhD degree in Computer Science and Engineering from Rabindranath Tagore University Bhopal (M.P.). His research includes Computer Network, Network Security, Cryptography, Data Mining. He is having 13 research publications in reputed International journal,International-National conferences and 6 - patents (2 published- 4 Registered), He is having 10 books international and national books in various domains, He also have qualified GATE (CSE) in 2015.

9 798890 024275

Printed by Libri Plureos GmbH in Hamburg,
Germany